THE BREASTFEEDING BLUEPRINT

How to Get Started and Keep It Flowing for a Year

Barbara L. Philipp, MD

Thank you to the moms and dads who helped others by allowing The Breastfeeding Blueprint to use your pictures.

Dedicated to

Mary Ellen Boisvert

a champion for mothers and babies

Her memory lives on in the maternity care she inspired.

Contents

Section 1

A Deeper Dive into Breast Milk

CHAPTER 01

Introduction

I WROTE THIS BOOK to share all I have learned about breastfeeding over the years and, hopefully, to help you on your breastfeeding journey.

One thing I know for sure is that the care you receive in the maternity hospital is key to your breastfeeding success. This is what I know best as for more than two decades I have either worked in or directed the newborn side of a maternity unit in Boston, Massachusetts. In retrospect, the care we used to provide supporting breastfeeding was poor. In 1995, the hospital where I worked had no lactation consultants, no breastfeeding classes, no breastfeeding education for maternity staff, and no policy that ensured breastfeeding women and infants would stay together after birth. The nursery was packed with rows of healthy newborns in bassinets. We didn't have many breastfeeders at the time – and, to be fair, we were doing what all the other hospitals were doing – but did a mother who came to our hospital wanting to breastfeed even have a chance?

Recognizing how unacceptable this was, we got to work. We formed a Task Force, examined policies, changed everything, and became the first Baby-Friendly hospital in Massachusetts and the 22nd in the nation in 1999. Since then we follow the Ten Steps to Successful Breastfeeding and offer a wealth of support and educational services around breastfeeding. Mothers and babies stay together. Staff members of the maternity unit are trained in breastfeeding medicine. Free formula samples, advertising, and the formula salesman have been banished from the hospital. Of course, we have formula, but we no longer accept it for free. The hospital pays Fair Market Value for it and formula products just like it does for IV bags, alcohol wipes, and gauze pads.

All these changes worked. Breastfeeding initiation rates at the hospital jumped from 58% (1995) to 87% (1999) to 92% (2019) and exclusive breastfeeding rates increased six-fold.

The Breastfeeding Blueprint explains not only why to do certain things but how to do them. It looks at why skin to skin in the first hour is so important and magical and how to safely do it. It looks at why rooming in with your infant as much as you can makes a difference. It provides a checklist to help you recognize your baby's nine instinctive stages, gives tips about the latch, and information about acceptable weight loss. There is a chapter on "normal," a description of the Gentle Cesarean Section, and a checklist on everything that will be done for the baby before you head for home. Tips are offered for succeeding when you get home and for when you head back to work. The book covers a wide range of topics, from lactation cookies to breast milk storage to donor milk.

This book also looks at obstacles to breastfeeding, from free formula samples given out in the obstetrician's office, to lack of workplace support, and strategies the 70-billion-dollar infant formula industry uses to try to get you to believe that formula and breast milk are the same (wrong!) I bet you will agree that it is not ok that breastfeeding mothers are hiding in corners, pumping in bathrooms, and getting kicked out of restaurants.

Breastfeeding for some is easy but for others it is like *The Hunger Games*, with one challenge after another. I so want you to meet your breastfeeding expectations and hope this book helps you. Remember the keys: be as prepared as you can be as you start the breastfeeding journey, pick a good hospital, move the milk, feed the baby, ask for help, ask for help again and again, and never quit on your worst day.

You got this, mama.

Barbara L. Philipp, MD, FAAP, FABM

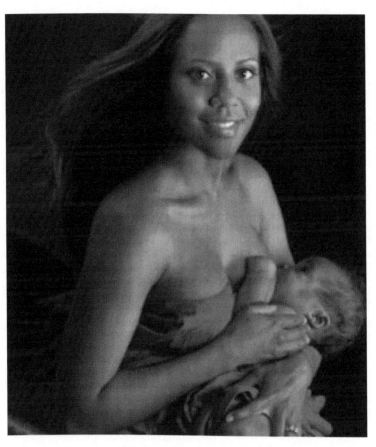

Photo: Best for Babes

CHAPTER 02

Babies Are Born to be Breastfed

BREASTFEEDING IS THE NORMAL way to feed a baby. Breast milk contains all the water, carbohydrates, proteins, fats, minerals, and vitamins the baby needs in the first six months of life – plus living cells, hormones, enzymes, immunoglobulins, and other substances that boost the baby's immune system, enhance brain development, and prime the baby for a healthy life. This complex fluid changes every day, according to the specific, individual needs of the baby.

Mothers who formula feed have a higher risk of:

- Breast cancer
- Ovarian cancer
- Type II diabetes
- Cardiovascular disease (heart attacks, strokes)

Formula-fed babies have a higher risk of:

- Ear infections
- Gastrointestinal illness (vomiting and diarrhea)
- Lower respiratory illness
- Obesity
- Sudden Infant Death Syndrome (SIDS)
- Type II diabetes
- Certain types of cancer (like leukemia)

What exactly is responsible for the difference in these health outcomes for breastfeeding dyads compared to formula-feeding dyads?

- Mother's milk is unique to the mammalian world and has evolved over millions of years to be species specific.

- The hooded seal's milk, at 60% fat, is the fattiest milk produced in the mammalian world. (Human milk, in comparison, is 3-5% fat.) The hooded seal lives about thirty years but spends only four days nursing, the shortest of any mammal. Seals live in the sea but must give birth and nurse out of the water, usually on floating sheets of ice. Adding drama to the event, the pups are born when the ice is beginning to melt and break up. The milk's high-fat content produces a thick layer of insulating blubber in her little pup. The seal pup *doubles* its weight in those four days.

- Rhinoceros milk has the lowest amount of fat content at .2%. Experts are not sure why, although some feel it may have something to do with their slow reproductive cycle.

- Australia's tammar wallabies produce sugar-rich milk for their joeys. The sugar content of 14% makes it one of the highest levels among mammals, and double the amount in human milk. Wallaby milk contains high levels of a particular sugar, oligosaccharides, which will be discussed at greater length below. It is thought that this special type of sugar may provide protection from infection for the joey when in the mother's pouch.

- The nine-banded armadillo produces milk with very high levels of calcium and phosphorus that are helpful in building a protective bony shell.

- Milk from the eastern cottontail rabbit is the most protein-rich among mammals at about 15%. The milk is also high in fat. These ingredients allow the mother to leave her young unattended for long periods of time. Cottontail mothers return to their nests to nurse their young only once a day. (Information from Seven of the Most Extreme Milks in the Animal Kingdom by Shreya Dasgupta, Smithsonian.

com, September 14, 2015.)

Human milk is even more complex than milk from other mammals.

Human milk helps the baby grow, but there is so much more. Human babies are born with immature immune systems making them highly susceptible to infections. Breast milk to the rescue as it is designed to offer intricate, layered, maximum infection protection. Then there is the human brain, growing and developing throughout the first one and one-half years of life. Once again, human milk is packed full of ingredients specially designed to grow the brain. It also appears that human milk puts babies on the healthiest pathway regarding illnesses much later on in life.

Whoever designed this amazing liquid should get an award. Let's try to understand it a bit better.

CHAPTER 03

Sugar Mama

THE SUGAR LACTOSE IS the main carbohydrate in human milk. It accounts for about 40% of the total calories provided by breast milk. Other types of sugars, called oligosaccharides, are also found in human milk and are drawing a lot of attention. So far scientists have identified more than 200 human milk oligosaccharides (HMOs). Two hundred! This makes HMOs the third most common ingredient in human breast milk (behind lactose and fats).

While it seems logical that the purpose of HMOs would be to provide the breastfeeding baby with a lot of energy, this is not the case. Scientists discovered that human newborns are unable to digest HMOs. The HMOs pass untouched, and undigested, through the stomach and the small intestine and end up in the large intestine where most of the bacteria in the gut microbiome are found.

Scientists then learned that HMOs serve as the food for bacteria in the large intestine, specifically a certain type of helpful bacteria called *Bifidobacteria*. The HMOs nourish the bacteria which allows them to grow and multiply (kind of like fertilizer). This explains the finding that the stool of breastfed babies contains more *Bifidobacteria* than the stool of formula-fed babies.

The plot thickens! One type of *Bifidobacteria*, *B. infantis*, has a particular affinity for the HMOs in breast milk. The HMOs and *B. infantis* join together to:

1) Stimulate gut development. As *B. infantis* eats HMOs, it releases short–chain fatty acids, which feed the infant's gut cells;

2) Provide protection from diseases. By directly touching infant gut cells, *B. infantis* causes them to stick together, blocking dangerous bacteria or viruses from passing through the little side alleys between the cells and entering the bloodstream; and

3) Boost brain development. After dining on HMOs, *B. infantis* releases a nutrient called sialic acid. Once absorbed from the gut into the blood stream, sialic acid participates in the growth of the baby's brain, which is growing incredibly fast in the first year of life.

With 200 HMOs in human milk, more findings will surely emerge about the important role each one of them plays in the baby's growth, health, and development.

Ed Yong. Breastfeeding the Microbiome.
The New Yorker. July 22, 2016.

Chapter 04

It's Alive

HUMAN MILK IS ALIVE, containing a variety of living white cells that fight infections. The different types of white blood cells include:

- Neutrophils
- Macrophages that gobble up bad bacteria. They also make the enzyme, lysozyme, which breaks up bacteria by disrupting the cell walls.
- Lymphocytes including both B cells and T cells. B cells produce antibodies. T cells can kill bad bacteria directly or send out messages to bring in other bacteria-fighting substances.

Colostrum, the first milk, contains 5 million white blood cells per milliliter (20 drops).

Pictured below is one drop of infant formula compared to one drop of human milk. The slides are stained blue so anything in the liquid can be seen. The dark circles in the human milk are different types of white blood cells. The white circles are fat globules that aid in development of the brain and eyes.

Under the Microscope: One Drop of Formula Compared to One Drop of Breast Milk

A Drop of Formula	A Drop of Breast Milk
	-White blood cells protect against infection -Fat globules help eyes and brain grow faster

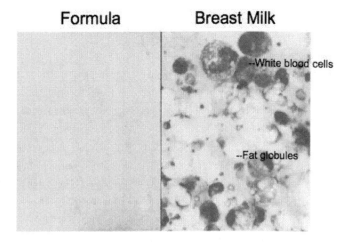

Human milk also contains stem cells, shown in below picture:

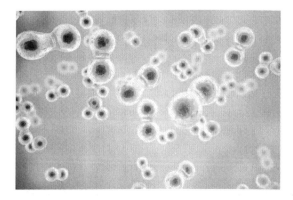

In comparison, infant formula contains no living products.

CHAPTER 05

Not Just Milk, It's Medicine

THE ARMY OF PROTECTION reporting for duty in human breast milk to fight infections includes:

- All classes of immunoglobulins (IgA, IgG, IgM, IgE, IgD)
- Bifid bacteria
- Resistance factor (protection against staphylococcal infection)
- Lysozyme
- Lactoferrin
- Complement
- Vitamin B12-binding protein
- Glycans and oligosaccharides
- Interleukins
- Cytokines
- Nucleotides
- Components in an immune response that is stimulated when baby saliva backwashes into the mammary tissue (read on)

Katie Hinde is a breast milk researcher who writes the blog, Mammals Suck ... Milk! In this piece entitled, Baby Spit Backwash, she gives an example of the complex relationship between mother and baby the infection protection that breast milk offers.

"Moms increase the concentration of some immunofactors in

breast milk when babies are sick (but moms are not).

When babies suckle, the nipple diameter increases and there is a vacuum with negative pressure that delivers fluids from the infant oral cavity – a cocktail of milk and saliva – back into the ducts of the breast. For the record, the technical term for 'baby spit backwash' is 'retrograde milk backflow.'

Milk is alive – with immune cells, stem cells, and microbes of maternal and infant origin.

Moreover, what we know about mammary gland anatomy and physiology and immune response indicates that this 'baby saliva stimulated immune response' is not so far-fetched.

Depending on the illness, babies shed pathogens from mucous membranes – upper respiratory nasties hitching a ride through runny noses and coughing mouths – mixing together in saliva and snot as babies latch on to suckle at the breast. These naso-oral secretions from the baby backwash into the nipple duct system, bringing the pathogens with them.

A fundamental component of the appropriately functioning immune system is that exposure to pathogens triggers immune responses. As any mother who has tangled with mastitis can tell you, immune response in the mammary gland is hecka important. And natural selection may have favored an increase in immune molecules in the mammary and milk because they function to protect the mammary gland, protect the baby, or both the mammary gland AND the baby.

Mother's milk is chock full of immune molecules. Babies rely on the immunological umbrella of their mother's breast milk while the baby's own immune system is naïve and developing – this is what makes milk not just food, but also medicine.

But get ready to be even more blown away!

When breast milk mixes with baby saliva, a chemical reaction happens that produces hydrogen peroxide. Yep – the combination of breast milk with baby saliva produces a strong enough reaction to 'inhibit growth of the opportunistic pathogens *Staphylococcus aureus* and *Salmonella spp*' while also promoting the growth of beneficial bacteria. Does adult saliva mixed with breast milk cause this reaction? Nope, just baby spit.

"This is just one of the myriad of ways that breastfeeding is a dynamic biological process, not simply a meal at the breast."

Written by Katie Hinde on her blog,
Mammals Suck... Milk!
Posted January 29, 2016

http://mammalssuck.blogpost.com/2016/01/breast-milk-baby-spit.html?m=1

CHAPTER 06

It's Dynamic

HUMAN BREAST MILK IS dynamic – constantly changing. Breast-milk changes during the day from one feeding to the next. It changes from one day to the next day and from one month to the next month. Human milk made for girls is different than milk made for boys. Milk made for premature infants is different than milk made for term newborns. The fat content of the first milk of the feed (foremilk) is lower than the fat content of the milk towards the end of the feed (hindmilk).

The first milk, colostrum, is protein packed goodness. Colostrum:

- Has a high concentration of antibodies, especially Secretory IgA, which coats and seals the gut, preventing harmful substances from getting into the bloodstream.

- Is very high in concentrated nutrition. A little bit goes a long way.

- Is high in carbohydrates and proteins and antibodies and low in fat, making it easy to digest.

- Has a laxative effect that helps the baby pass meconium that prevents newborn jaundice.

In comparison, infant formula is the exact same product from one bottle to the next.

Chapter 07

It's Location Specific

A SPECIAL TYPE OF tissue called Gut Associated Lymphoid Tissue (GALT) is found all along the gut. When harmful bacteria or viruses from the mother's environment enter her gut, cells in GALT make antibodies (in the form of IgA) directly targeted to the harmful agents. The IgA travels to the mammary gland. Upon reaching the mammary gland a switcheroo happens where IgA is transformed into Secretory IgA. Secretory IgA is not digested by stomach acids nor digested in the gut. Therefore, it remains in the lumen, coating the gut cells along the way. This special circuit, from the mother's gut to mother's milk, is called the entero-mammary pathway.

Knowing this, would you ever tell a mother to stop breast-feeding if she is sick? No! Her breast milk is the one thing that is going to protect her baby from her illness. Would it make sense for the mother to go sit in the baby's daycare center a few days before her baby's daycare starts and give all the other babies there a hug and a kiss? It might, because her breast milk coud quickly contain antibodies targeted at the germs in the daycare center.

CHAPTER 08

It's Packed with Powerful Proteins

PROTEINS IN BREAST MILK make up hormones, enzymes, and antibodies. Hormones in breast milk include prolactin, thyroid hormones, growth factors, relaxin, endorphins, erythropoietin, cortisol, leptin, estrogen, and progesterone.

In comparison, infant formula contains no hormones, no enzymes, and no antibodies.

Casein and whey are two other proteins in milk. Casein forms a curd; whey is in the liquid portion. The ratio of casein to whey in formula is 80:20; the ratio of casein to whey in breast milk is 40:60. Due to more clumpy curd that is difficult to digest, formula fed babies are often constipated. Breastfed babies are rarely constipated.

Another important protein found in human milk, lactoferrin, has the ability to bind to iron in the gut, making it unavailable for bad bacteria. Bad bacteria in the gut feed and grow with the help of iron.

Chapter 09

It's Full of Fabulous Fats

Human milk by percentage of concentration is #1 lactose, #2 fats, #3 HMOs. Fats serve as the main source of energy. They also are carriers of fat-soluble vitamins that provide essential omega-3 and omega-6 fatty acids. In human milk, 50% of calories are supplied by fats, mostly in the form of triglycerides of saturated and unsaturated origin. Two hundred fatty acids have been identified in human milk lipids, with 50 being metabolically active. The major fatty acids are palmitic, stearic, oleic, and linoleic with omega-6 (linoleic acid) and omega-3 (alpha-linolenic acid) fatty acids. Breast milk contains another long-chain fatty acid, eicosapentanoic acid (EPA). Breast milk also contains cholesterol, an essential component of all membranes.

The alveolar cells in the mammary gland manufacture and secret fat into the breastmilk. Each fat droplet consists of a triglyceride (fatty) center, surrounded by a unique triple membrane called Milk Fat Globule Membrane (MFGM). MFGM is made up a diverse group of proteins, some lipids, and minor bioactive sterols. Products of the fat in the droplet include DHA and ARA. The fat complex in human milk is especially important for brain development and cognitive function.

DHA (decosahexanoic acid) is in human milk, but the amount present depends on the mother's dietary intake. DHA is the most abundant omega-3 long-chain fatty acid in the brain, making up 40-50% of the polyunsaturated fatty acids (PUFAs). In addition, 50% of the weight of a neuron's plasma membrane is composed of DHA. About 40% of the retina is made of DHA. It is also an important component in skin, sperm, and testicles. The recommendation for pregnant and lactating woman is to take 300 mg a day of DHA.

ARA (arachidonic acid) is another polyunsaturated fatty acid – this one omega 3 – naturally synthesized by the body from linoleic acid. It plays an important role in the infant's growth.

Fat content in human milk is highly variable, changing over a feeding, from one breast to the other, over a day's time, over time, and among individuals. In this picture of pumped breast milk, the fat separated and is floating on top, which is totally normal. Just give it a swirl and you are good to go.

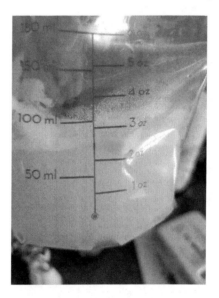

In this bag of pumped breast milk, the fat component is floating on top.

During the first year of life, the human brain more than doubles in size. Of this growth, 85% is cerebrum and 50-60% of the solid matter is lipid.

Components in human milk are specially designed to feed and grow the brain.

In comparison, the fat in infant formula comes from a blend of vegetable oils.

John Medina in his book, *Brain Rules for Babies: How to Raise a Smart and Happy Child from Zero to Five*, sums it up, "If America knew what breast milk can do for the brains of its youngest citizens, lactating mothers across the nation would be enshrined, not embarrassed ... If we as a country wanted a smarter population, we would insist on lactation rooms in every public establishment. A sign would hang from the door of these rooms, Quiet please. Brain development in progress."

CHAPTER 10

The Debate is Over

IT SEEMS LIKE THERE is plenty of proof to support the 2009 statement by David Meyers, MD, from the Agency for Healthcare Research and Quality that the debate about what to feed a newborn is over.

"The debate is over about the importance of breastfeeding for healthy outcomes for women and children in the United States. There is no debate. We don't need any more evidence in order to reach a conclusion about whether or not breastfeeding has important health outcomes that matter for the individual and for the population of children and women in this country. The real questions are:

- How do we support women and families in breastfeeding and exclusively breastfeeding?
- What can the healthcare system itself do?
- What is our responsibility?
- How are we currently supporting it, and how are we currently sabotaging it?
- What can employers do?
- What can society in general do?
- What can policy makers and the government do?"

Dr. Nigel Rollins from the World Health Organization agrees that it takes a village to breastfeed:

"The success or failure of breastfeeding should not be seen solely as the responsibility of the woman. Her ability to breast-feed is very much shaped by the support and the environment in which she lives. There is a broader responsibility of governments and society to support women through policies and programmes in the community."

CHAPTER 11

Breastfeed for How Long – What do the Experts Say?

THE DEFINITION OF EXCLUSIVE breastfeeding is an infant's consumption of human milk with no other liquids or solids except for drops or syrups of vitamins, minerals and medications.

Pediatricians, obstetricians and family medicine doctors are all in agreement in their recommendations about exclusivity and duration of breastfeeding.

The American Academy of Pediatrics (AAP) recommends exclusive breastfeeding for about six months, followed by continued breastfeeding as complementary foods are introduced, with continuation of breastfeeding for one year or longer as mutually desired by mother and infant.

The AAP describes breastfeeding and human milk as "the normative standards for infant feeding and nutrition" and further states, given the documented short and long-term medical and neurodevelopmental advantages of breastfeeding, infant nutrition should be considered a public health issue and not only a lifestyle choice."

Section on Breastfeeding, American Academy of Pediatrics
Breastfeeding and the Use of Human Milk
Pediatrics 2012;129:e827–e841

The American College of Obstetricians and Gynecologists (ACOG) recommends "exclusive breastfeeding for the first six months of life, with continued breastfeeding as complementary foods are introduced through the infant's first year of life, or longer as mutually desired by the woman and her infant." ACOG Committee on Obstetric Practice. Committee Opinion. Optimizing support for breastfeeding as part of obstetric practice. Number 658;February 2016.

The American Academy of Family Physicians (AAFP) recommends exclusive breastfeeding for six months, breastfeeding beyond the first year as long as mutually desired and add solid foods at six months. The AAFP advocates for the doctor to act as a strong supporter of breastfeeding. http://www.aafp.org/about/policies/all/breastfeeding-support.html 2017

In the perfect world women would exclusively breastfeed for six months and keep it going for a year or more. But breastfeeding can be hard, and the demands of life can make reaching those goals difficult. Therefore, do the best you can. One day of breastfeeding is better than none, two days are better than one, and three are better than two. Consider these tips:

- Pick a good maternity hospital.
- Safety first. Feed the baby.
- Understand that this may be hard.
- Ask for help and, if you really want to meet these goals, never quit on your hardest day.

Section 2

Birth, Baby and Hospital Days: Tips to
Get Off to a Great Start

CHAPTER 12A

Skin-to-Skin Contact

WHAT HAPPENS IN THE maternity hospital matters because the first days are critical for breastfeeding success. Some maternity hospitals, like the hospital where I work in Boston, Massachusetts have worked hard to change, and we continue working to offer the best evidence-based maternity care. Some hospitals have not changed, so be aware that you may need to speak up and demand the type of care described in this book.

Skin-to-skin is the best way to begin. Skin-to-skin contact is the practice of placing the newborn in direct contact with the mother (or caregiver) right after birth. The newborn, naked or wearing only a diaper (hat optional), is placed so the front side of the newborn is touching the naked chest of the mother. A blanket is placed on the baby's back.

For vaginal births, the recommendation is for immediate and uninterrupted skin-to-skin contact in the immediate post-partum period at least until the first breastfeed or for one hour for the formula-feeding mother or for as long as the mother wishes. Maternity staff is expected to help the mother recognize when the baby is ready to breastfeed and help with the latch and feed.

Skin-to-skin contact with the mother who has had a Cesarean birth is recommended when the mother is stable and alert and then it should last for an uninterrupted hour. More information about Cesarean births is provided below.

It is amazing how hard it can be for maternity staff to leave the mother and baby alone for an hour after an uncomplicated birth.

They have a lot of tasks to complete and may be worrying about their work backing up. Allowing the baby to adapt to his/her new environment takes time and a hands-off approach (other than very close observation, of course). Skin-to-skin contact in the first hour of life is the critical first step to breastfeeding success.

Skin-to-skin contact is magic. It:

- Promotes bonding;
- Helps breastfeeding;
- Is associated with less crying in the baby;
- Stabilizes the baby's sugar level;
- Regulates the baby's vital signs: heart rate, respiratory rate and temperature; and
- Normalizes a Cesarean birth.

Checklist: The Newborn's Nine Instinctive Stages

A BABY IS BORN ready to interact with the mother and knows exactly what to do after birth. An infant placed on the mother's abdomen immediately after birth exhibits nine instinctive stages of innate newborn behavior.

1. Birth cry
   o Hello world! The lungs expand with your baby's first cry.
2. Relaxation (lasts 2-3 minutes)
   o The baby is very quiet and still.
3. Awakening (about 3 minutes)
   o The head and shoulders move, the baby may open his eyes and make small mouthing movements.
4. Activity (about 8 minutes)
   o The eyes remain open; the baby may look for his mother. The baby exhibits increased mouthing and suckling, with increase saliva production.
5. Resting
   o Rest periods may occur at any time between other stages.
6. Crawling (at about 20 minutes)
   o The baby begins to approach the breast by leaping, crawling, sliding, and/or pushing. The kicking motion

of the feet may help deliver the placenta. The baby continues mouthing and suckling movements even though he is not ready to latch.

7. Familiarization (about 45 minutes)
    o The baby may lick, touch or massage the breast while looking at the mother. The baby may rub his own face and mouth with his hands.

8. Suckling (about 60 minutes)
    o The baby self-attaches to the nipple and begins to suck with minimal or no assistance. This may take longer if the baby was exposed to analgesia or anesthesia.

9. Sleeping (90-120 minutes)
    o The baby and sometimes the mother fall into a deep sleep.

In one study, infants that sought out the breast and "self attached" developed better sucking techniques than infants in the control group who were removed from the mother after twenty minutes for routine hospital procedures. In another study of ten infants placed skin-to-skin after vaginal births to mothers who were not exposed to any maternal analgesia, infants used their hands to reach for, explore, and stimulate their mother's breast in preparation for the first breastfeeding. Infant hand movements and sucking patterns were found to be coordinated. An increase in levels of maternal oxytocin was associated with periods of increased hand massage or sucking of the breast.

In summary, infants who breastfeed in the first hour of life have a better suck and increased breastfeeding duration compared with infants whose first breastfeeding is delayed.

Also, the American College of Obstetricians and Gynecologists (ACOG) recommends delaying cord clamping for 30-60 seconds after birth. Others suggest longer, until the cord stops pulsating. Benefits of delayed cord clamping for the baby include receiving more red blood cells (decreasing the risk of anemia later on), more immune factors, and more stem cells.

This is a picture of my daughter, Jess, and my grandson, Anthony, enjoying skin-to-skin contact in the first hour.

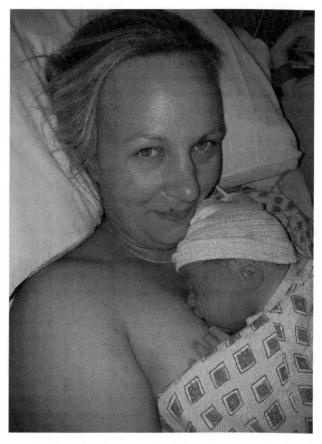

Here Wendy, Jess' longtime childhood friend, and her son, Jamieson, enjoy skin-to-skin contact in the first hour. Dad took this picture and was watching the baby's mouth and nose.

CHAPTER 12c

Frequently Asked Questions

Q. After birth, what happens after an hour or more of skin-to-skin contact?

A. Newborns and mothers are wide-awake for several hours after birth and then both fall into a deep sleep for hours. This is why keeping visitors away for at least 12 hours after birth (ideally 24 hours in my opinion) is a great idea.

Q. What if the baby is sick and needs extra attention?

A. If this happens, the baby will be taken to the "warmer," a piece of equipment usually located in the corner of the birthing room. Once stable, the baby can be returned to the mother for skin-to-skin holding, which then should be for an uninterrupted hour or until the first feed.

Q. What if the mother is sick after the birth?

A. In that case, the baby's father or another support person can be encouraged to hold the baby skin-to-skin. This might happen in the delivery room, the operating room, or in the nursery. Again, the goal is that once started, the skin-to-skin holding will last for an uninterrupted hour.

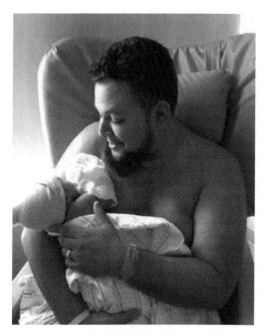

A dad sees his baby's eyes for the first time.

Q. What if you don't want to breastfeed?

A. Skin-to-skin contact is recommended for all babies.

Q. What if the baby arrives early?

A. A premature infant, defined as being born at less than 36 weeks gestation, may need to be admitted immediately to the Special Care Nursery (SCN) or Neonatal Intensive Care Unit (NICU). The mother should be helped with hand expression or pumping as soon as possible once she is stable. Any drops of colostrum can be collected, taken to the NICU, and swabbed into the baby's mouth. Once the baby is stabilized, kangaroo care (which is what skin-to-skin contact is called in the NICU) is encouraged.

Q. What if you have a Cesarean birth?

A. With a national Cesarean rate of about 35%, there is a one in three chance that this might happen.

- For decades, babies and mothers were immediately separated after a Cesarean section. Once the baby was born, the baby went to the nursery. The obstetrician completed the mother's surgery and she was then moved to a special post-surgical area (often called the Post Anesthesia Care Unit or PACU). Eventually the mother and the baby were reunited but this frequently occurred hours later.

- Hospitals are now working to make the Cesarean section birth more family centered. The goal of the new movement, called the Gentle Cesarean Section, is for the mother to experience the birth of her baby. The components of the Gentle Cesarean Section are:

  1. A clear drape is used to delineate the surgical area so the mother can see the birth of the baby;
  2. The monitor leads are moved to the mother's back so her chest is clear and ready for skin-to-skin contact;
  3. Instead of both arms being restrained, one arm is freed up; and
  4. Skin-to-skin contact in the Operating Room is encouraged.

- You may wonder why Gentle Cesarean Sections aren't always done, as they sound so much better, right? Obstacles are numerous: the obstetrician may not be comfortable with the idea, the anesthesiologist might not be on board, or nursing staffing could be inadequate. The birth of a baby means another patient has arrived in the operating room (OR) and a nurse needs to come into the OR specifically to watch the baby. This has financial and staffing implications for the unit. Ask if your hospital does Gentle Cesarean Sections. If not, and you would like this, tell them that is what you want. But remember, safety trumps everything. The goal is for the baby to be healthy and get out safely, and to ensure the mother is stable and able. Only then think about skin-to-skin holding.

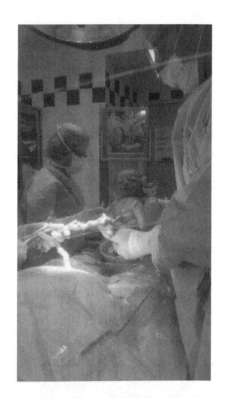

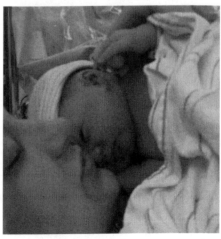

Pictures of a "Gentle C-Section"

Many hospitals now "wait for the weight" (wait to obtain the birth weight) for an hour to allow the baby to be in skin-to-skin contact for an uninterrupted hour.

Then, skin-to-skin holding should be encouraged throughout the maternity stay. The American Academy of Pediatrics (AAP) recommends "direct skin-to-skin contact with mothers immediately after delivery until the first feeding is accomplished" and encourages it to continue "throughout the postpartum period."

Chapter 12d

Safety First – Always!

REPORTS HAVE BEEN PUBLISHED of infants collapsing after birth while being held in skin-to-skin contact, a condition called Sudden Unexpected Postnatal Collapse (SUPC).

Risk factors of SUPC include: Apgar <7 at 5 minutes, medical complications at birth, late preterm infant (34.0 weeks to 36.6 weeks), a complicated delivery (vacuum, forceps, prolonged second stage), a mother on narcotics or having received general anesthesia, an extremely sleepy or sedated mother, a mother who is obese or has large, pendulous breasts, and a mother talking on a cell phone. SUPC is rare, but it does happen. Maternity unit staff will be carefully monitoring both mother and baby.

To prevent SUPC, care should be taken to practice proper positioning. The mother should be in a somewhat upright position when holding her newborn in skin-to-skin contact. For the baby, be sure:

- The face can be seen.
- The head in the "sniffing" position (nose and chin up).
- The nose and mouth are not covered, the head is turned to one side, and the neck is straight (not bent or kinked).
- The shoulders and chest are flat against the mother's chest.
- The legs are flexed and the back is covered with blankets.

Safe Positioning for Skin-to-Skin

Mother:

- Somewhat upright, not flat

Infant:

- Face can be seen
- Nose and mouth not covered. Head turned to one side.
- Head in "sniffing" position
- Neck is straight, not bent

P.S. Dad took this picture and could see the baby's mouth and nose.

Example of Unsafe Skin-to-Skin

Problems here:

- Mother is too flat, sleepy, unable to see baby's face
- Baby's head not in a "sniffing" position
- Baby's mouth and nose are covered

Next Step: Wake mom and/or place baby in own sleep space

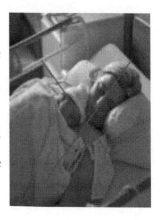

Hormones

When the baby suckles at the breast, signals are sent to the pituitary gland in the brain and two important hormones are secreted. Prolactin instructs mammary cells in the breast to make the milk. Oxytocin directs muscle fibers in the mammary tissue to contract, causing the letdown reflex and pushing the milk out. Oxytocin also signals muscle fibers in the uterus to contract which helps control the amount of uterine bleeding. Uterine cramping while breastfeeding is a sign of a good latch!

Oxytocin is also known as the love hormone. With birth, skin-to-skin holding, and breastfeeding, the mother's level of oxytocin surges causing a flood of emotions and overwhelming feelings for her new baby. She shifts to being more "right brained" – more emotional than rational, less analytical, living in the moment, feeling like now is forever, and feeling like she's in a Zen-like state. This allows the mother to be in synchrony with her baby.

CHAPTER 13

Hello Baby!

Now that the baby is here – the hospital has a new patient. Newborn procedures in the first hours of life include:

- Frequent vital signs
- Application of the identification band
- Application of the security band
- Apgar scores
- Quick physical examination
- Eye ointment
- Vitamin K shot
- Birth weight

Of the newborn procedures, only the assignment of the Apgar scores and vital signs are immediately time-dependent, and these can be done with the baby skin-to-skin on the mother's abdomen or chest. Application of an identification band and security band can also take place with the baby held skin-to-skin.

The Apgar score

Virginia Apgar, MD (1909-1974) was an American obstetrical anesthesiologist who invented the Apgar score, a way to quickly assess the health of the newborn immediately after birth. An Apgar score is assigned at one and five minutes of life (and also sometimes at 10 minutes). The score assesses the baby's state during the transition period, the first minutes of life when the baby adapts to living outside the womb. A baby's "Apgar" is determined by five criteria, with a maximum of two points assigned for each category. Each letter stands for something: A (appearance), P (pulse), G (grimace), A (activity), and R (respiration). "8 and 9" is a common score, indicating 8 at one minute and 9 at five minutes. It is highly unusual for a baby to receive "10 and 10" because almost all babies are born with a bluish color to the skin.

Score	0	1	2
Appearance (color)	Blue, pale	Extremities blue	Completely pink
Pulse (heart rate per min)	Absent	<100	>100
Grimace	No response	Grimace	Cough, sneeze
Activity (tone)	Limp	Extremity flexion	Active motion
Respiratory effort	Absent, irregular	Slow, crying	Good

Wait for the weight

Obtaining the baby's birth weight should be delayed until the first breastfeeding feeding is completed or for an hour for the mother who intends to formula feed. Parents need to know ahead of time that this is the plan. The goal is for skin-to-skin contact to be uninterrupted for at least an hour and then the weight can be obtained and the physical exam is completed (which is different than the APGAR score). Once again, we are talking about a healthy baby. Safety first.

Eyes and thighs

"Eyes" refers to the eye ointment applied to protect the baby against neonatal conjunctivitis. The ointment is applied in a small ribbon and remains until it naturally dissolves. "Thighs" refers to the shot of Vitamin K given to protect against bleeding in the brain. The timing of the eye ointment is usually determined by the state's Department of Public Health. Unfortunately, those regulations are often dated. The current recommendations from the American Academy of Pediatrics are to delay eye prophylaxis until after the first feed is completed and delay administration of the intramuscular vitamin K shot until "after the first feeding is completed but within six hours of birth."

Admission examination

A more complete physical examination of the baby, including length and head circumference measurements, is often completed later on. AWHONN, the Association of Women's Health, Obstetric and Neonatal Nurses, recommends that the thorough physical examination be done by four hours of life and nursing protocols at many hospitals follow their rules. AWHONN does NOT say that the newborn admission exam needs to be done right away.

CHAPTER 14

Rooming-In

ROOMING-IN REFERS TO THE location of the baby on the maternity unit. The definition of rooming-in is that the newborn is with the mother, in her room, 24 hours each day.

With rooming-in, together is the standard of care. Separation occurs for staff-initiated reasons – medical conditions or issues like: circumcision, tongue-tie clips, antibiotic administration, or a car seat test (if needed). The expectation is that the baby is out of the mother's room for less than one hour a day (again for staff-initiated reasons). Other than that, everything is done for the baby with the baby in the mother's room.

Rooming-in is important because it:

1. Promotes bonding

2. Encourages on demand feeding, helps breastfeeding

3. Allows a mother to watch for and learn about her infant's feeding cues

4. Helps a mother learn how to handle and comfort her baby

5. Eliminates baby-mix ups (baby brought back to the wrong room)

Historical Look

Rooming in is a BIG change in practice. To get an appreciation for just how big, take a look at the following instruction sheet given to mothers in a US maternity ward in 1968:

INSTRUCTIONS (circa 1968)

1. Babies are on display at Nursery window from 2:30 to 3:30 P.M. and 7:00 to 7:45 P.M. Please do not ask to see baby at any other time.

2. Baby will come to mother for feeding 9-10 A.M., 1-2 P.M., 5:30-6:30 P.M., 9-10 P.M. (No visitor is allowed on floor or in room during nursing periods, including father.)

3. Do not smoke while baby is in the room.

4. Do not allow visitors to sit on your bed. (The bed linen must be clean for the baby.)

5. Do not cover your baby with your linen.

Even in the 1980's when I was a pediatric resident training in Boston, the standard of care was that babies would be whisked away to the nursery right after birth ("the nursery pit stop"). In the nursery, the nurse and doctor would complete their admission examinations and paper work in an orderly fashion. The entire system was set up with the nurse and doctor in mind, not the mother and baby. The nursery was a busy place with rows and rows of babies in bassinettes. One nurse was assigned to care for the mother in her room and a separate nurse, the nursery nurse, was assigned to care for the baby. This was just the way it was at most hospitals for decades.

With the shift to rooming in, the baby's room is the mother's room. The healthy baby never goes to the nursery as everything is done for the baby in the mother's room. The same nurse cares for the mother and the baby in the mother's room (this is called couplet care). The nursery is a quiet place, only for the baby who may be having trouble with transitioning or if the mother is sick or out of the room (example: getting a tubal ligation). In a hospital where rooming-in is practiced, it would not be unusual to see an empty nursery. If you have a healthy baby, you may never even know where the nursery is.

A rooming-in policy protects the rights of the mother and baby to be together. A hospital that practices rooming-in has worked hard to change practice since it is much easier for maternity hospital staff to get their work done with a system in place that drives all the healthy babies into the nursery for examinations, screenings and procedures.

If you find you need a break and YOU would like the baby to go to the nursery for a while, talk about that with your nurse, come up with a plan, and it can happen. Some mothers will ask for the baby to go to the nursery for a while at night, with the plan that if the baby shows feeding cues that the baby will be brought back to the mother's room to feed.

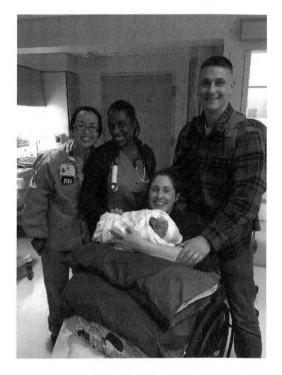

Jess, Phil and Anthony (only hours old) get ready to go to Jess' room on the Mother Baby Unit. The hospital practices rooming in so there was no "nursery pit stop" for Anthony. His room was his mother's room. Thank you to the *awesome* Labor and Delivery staff.

CHAPTER 15

Newborn procedures

BELOW IS A LIST OF newborn procedures that need to be completed before the baby goes home. All of these can be done with the baby in the mother's room:

- Daily weights
- Frequent vital signs
- Daily examinations
- Newborn bath (usually one)
- Newborn pictures
- Hepatitis B shot
- Newborn metabolic screen (a blood draw obtained by pricking the baby's heel)
- Bilirubin screen (a blood draw to check for jaundice)
- Hearing test (a little probe is placed in each ear)
- Heart test (a little probe is placed on the baby's right hand and right foot to measure oxygen saturation)
- Red reflex (checking the eyes to look at the retinas)
- Discharge exam

Delay the Bath

Many hospitals now are "delaying the bath." At Boston Medical Center, we used to bathe babies around two hours of life because they were all in the nursery and it was a good time to get that task completed. However, that was the probably the worst time for a bath as it would stress and chill the baby at the exact time when its blood sugar was at its lowest point. Following the bath, the baby's temperature dropped so the baby needed to go to the warmer. The baby might become jittery, having a blood sugar that was low. Then the baby was fed formula from a bottle to stabilize the blood sugar.

We learned there is no need to bathe babies so quickly. Many hospitals are delaying the bath to 12-24 hours or even longer than 24 hours which allows the baby to stay warm and the blood sugar to stay in a normal and safe range. Some hospitals don't bathe babies at all, and report that leaving the vernix on (the protective white coating on the skin) decreases dryness and cracking.

You decide what you would like for your baby.

Below is the information given to families about delay the bath at a Boston maternity hospital.

The First Bath

Your baby will have his/her first bath after 12-24 hours of life. Delaying the bath helps your baby stay warm and keeps the blood sugar in a normal and safe range.

CHAPTER 16

Baby Plan

I GAVE BIRTH TO my oldest daughter in 1984, and in 1989 along came twins, a boy and a girl. Despite being a board-certified pediatrician at the time, I knew not much at all about breast-feeding and assumed (incorrectly) that the maternity hospital knew what they were doing to support breastfeeding. Now, I know a lot about breastfeeding and how to support it. So, if I could turn back time and do it again, this is what I would do.

First, if I could I would get my care from a midwife who works in a Baby-Friendly designated hospital. If might consider hiring a Doula. I would let my employer know I plan on being gone for six months after the birth of the baby and when I return, I would be needing time out of my schedule several times a day to pump and a really nice, private place to pump that is close to the clinic.

Below is the procedure or test followed by what I would ask for (assuming baby is stable and healthy – safety first!):

Cord Clamping
- I would request that this be delayed.

Apgar scores
- Please obtain while being held skin-to-skin.

Vital signs, identification bands, safety tags
- Obtain or apply while the baby is being held skin-to-skin.

Uninterrupted skin-to-skin holding for at least 1-2 hours is important to me

- Yes

Waiting for the first weight is important to me
- Yes

Eyes (This refers to ointment applied to baby's eyes by two hours of life)
- The American Academy of Pediatrics recommends this but I hate the thought of blinding the baby so early on. I would ask that it be delayed until the baby has been held skin to skin and latched on.

Thighs (This refers to the Vitamin K shot given to protect infant from bleeding into the brain.)
- Yes, but to be given towards the end of two hours of life.

Full RN physical examination of the baby
- I request this be done in the mother's room at 3-4 hours of life.

Any nurse and MD caring for us must have had training on lactation.
- Not an issue if birthing at a Baby-Friendly hospital.

All items listed below should be done in my post partum room:

Hepatitis B shot (given <12 hours of life)
- The AAP and CDC recommend this be given <12 hours of life. We are noticing mothers with negative Hepatitis B Surface Antigen screens are declining this while in the maternity hospital and then getting it at the first newborn appointment.

Newborn metabolic screen (blood obtained on the second morning by pricking the baby's heel)
- Yes

Bilirubin screen (blood obtained at same time as metabolic screen)
- Yes

Hearing screen (a small device is gently placed in each of the baby's ears)
- Yes

Heart screen (done when the baby is greater than 24 hours old by placing a small probe on the baby's hand and foot)

- Yes

Daily weights and MD exams of baby in mother's room

- Yes

Newborn bath

- Yes, please teach me how to do a bath but we do not want it done before the baby is 24 ours old.

Birth certificate

- I am aware I need to provide information for this.

Circumcision (if boy)

- Yes
- To be done only by attending physician with parent present

If the baby has a tongue-tie that needs to be clipped, parent to be present

- Yes

I will consent to donor milk if needed

- Yes

I am also requesting:

- No infant formula without consent of parents
- Please honor Quiet Time

Baby follow/up appointment will be at_____, with_____.

Chapter 17

Normal – A Letter To You

Dear Mama-to-Be,

IN A FEW WEEKS you are going to have a baby. These are exciting times! You have stated that you want to breastfeed, which of course is great, but I have to share that I wonder how it will go because with breastfeeding there are unknowns. I am writing you this letter so you will know what is normal and, as knowledge is power, have the best chance at breastfeeding success.

Unfortunately, we live in a society that is not supportive of breastfeeding. It makes me sad to say this, but it is true. Messages on social media, free gifts in the mail, and unwanted computer pop-ups set certain expectations about feeding a baby. The images imply that, for the mother, breastfeeding is like walking in a sun-splashed, flower-filled, lush meadow wearing a white billowing dress with perfectly coiffed hair holding an adorable, smiling, chubby baby. It really doesn't work that way.

The formula culture we live in influences what many people think about feeding. Get ready for this, as people will not hesitate to offer their opinions. Many think that babies eat 6-8 ounces of formula every three or four hours like clockwork (and the one-day old newborn definitely MUST drink a full 2 oz. bottle every three hours). But here's the deal. Breastfeeding babies and formula feeding babies are different. Breastfeeding babies eat smaller volumes and feed more frequently than formula feeding babies. This is normal.

Your body has been preparing to breastfeed throughout your pregnancy. Once the placenta is delivered, some hormone levels drop and other hormone levels rise, and this turns the breast milk production switch to the full-on position.

Labor probably will be hard for you and it will be hard for the baby, too. Sometimes we forget what it is like for the baby. Imagine the stress when he pops out into his new world for the first time: the loud sounds, the bright lights, and all the strange people. He is going to take his first breath ever. He is going to see you for the first time ever. He is going to eat his first meal all by himself ever. He has a lot of work to do and he is so little. This is why skin-to-skin contact and being close to you is normal. The nursery, so far away from you, is not normal and is incredibly stressful to the new baby.

This little guy's immune system is extremely immature. Your breast milk, even though it may seem like just drops in the beginning, is his infection protection. It is so important. No matter the circumstances — see if at the very least you can hand express colostrum onto a spoon to be fed to the baby.

Breastfeeding is the normal way to feed a baby. With breast-feeding, moving the milk is key.

Removing the milk from the breast signals the brain to make more milk. A breast full of milk actually has a protein-like substance building up that sends STOP making the milk signals to the brain. For some new moms, all that is needed to move the milk is the baby. But sometimes early on, the baby may be sleepy, or born a few weeks early and is pokey, or is trying but having trouble with his suck. These things can be fixed but might take some time. In the meantime you need to move the milk and the tricks that you have up your sleeve are: hand compression when the baby is breastfeeding, hand expression before or after the baby feeds, and the electric breast pump. You might never need to use the electric pump in the first weeks — who knows, we shall see — but it will be sitting in the corner of your room if you need it.

Don't worry if you try hand expression and the first few times nothing comes out. Often the first 24 hours using the breast pump nothing comes out. This can be normal. The important thing is the repeated stimulation to the breast that tells the brain to kick in and make the milk.

Moving the milk over and over and over again is key. It's a demand and supply, demand and supply type of thing. The first day of breastfeeding is different than the second day, the first week is different than the second week, and the first month is different than the second month. Eventually your body will make plenty of milk but in the early days you are placing your order.

The baby is your buddy on this journey. His tummy is small in the first weeks (blueberry – grape – strawberry – lime) so he will want to eat frequently. Actually, it may seem like he wants to eat all the time. This is normal. He will tell you when he wants to eat. Watch for feeding cues, sucking on the hand or fist, smacking lips, and moving around. Remember to "watch the baby, not the clock."

It's easiest to feed a calm baby when he shows early feeding cues. If he gets upset, remember, your bare chest is a calming place for the baby.

At work, I wear a button on the lapel of my white coat that says, "8 or more in 24." The saying is catchy but perhaps not totally accurate. Breastfeeding babies often feed more than 8 feeds in 24 hours – think more in the range of 11-16 times in 24 hours. This is called feeding on demand. The #1 ingredient in human milk is the sugar lactose; the higher the lactose content in milk, the more frequent the feeds. Therefore the formula-feeding idea of feeding a newborn every three to four hours is nonsense. Frequent feeding is normal.

The first day is a little different than subsequent days. You will be tired after the birth and the baby will be tired too. After the first several hours of skin-to-skin and the first feed, moms and babies often go into a deep sleep for up to ten hours. The first day the feeds might be six times and that is normal. The first milk, colostrum, is so important as to be mentioned twice → it is infection protection.

A newborn does this thing called cluster feeding. He eats, you put him down, and he wants to eat again. You feed him, put him down, and he will want to eat again. The baby is doing his job, working to drive up your milk supply. This is normal. Cluster feeds don't last forever. Once your milk supply ramps up, the baby will be much more content with feeds.

Babies lose weight in the first few days as they are born with extra fluid onboard. This is normal. The doctor taking care of the baby will keep an eye on this while you help by counting the pees and poops. The poops go from meconium (black, tarry) to the color of mud-pie filling (brown) to breast-milk stools (loose, looking like French's mustard with cottage cheese). Once you get into a rhythm, the baby may poop after every breastfeed. This is normal.

The baby losing weight early on does NOT mean you are not making enough milk. Colostrum is what comes in at the beginning and its contents lead me to believe (one more time) that it really is about infection protection for the baby – then, after a few days, much more milk will come in. This is normal.

The breastfeeding journey is about moving the milk, but it is also about the latch, the way the baby attaches to your breast to transfer milk. The nurses, doctors and lactation consultants will be helping you get an asymmetric latch and showing you how to do hand compression and hand expression. Learn about how to do laid-back breastfeeding. This whole thing is like learning to dance with a partner for the first time. The first few times out on the dance floor toes get stepped on (this is normal) but eventually it becomes a beautiful rhythm and you and the baby will be doing the cha-cha.

Back to hormones again – sucking at the breast increases prolactin levels. Sucking at the breast AT NIGHT increases prolactin levels even higher. The higher your prolactin levels, the more milk you will make. Therefore, a trick is to sleep when you can during the day (take advantage of Quiet Time) to be ready for the night feeds. Being up at night breastfeeding is normal.

If the baby gets a bottle of formula, you are not moving your milk. When a baby sucks on a pacifier, you are not moving your milk. We will get to pacifiers and bottles later on in this book, but in the beginning, they can both make things worse. Those poor overfed formula feeding babies – filling up a newborn's stomach that doesn't stretch out like an adult's stomach, to the point he is throwing up, IS NOT normal.

All this will come after you have labored for who knows how long and are exhausted. Talk about super powers! You are probably going to feel like you are in a brain fog. This is normal. Tina Smillie taught me that new mothers shift to right brained thinking so they can be in synchrony with their baby. Just go with it, enjoy it. Your regular brain will come back, I promise.

I suggest that every time you feed the baby in the first few days ask the nurse or doctor to take a look at the latch. How are you supposed to know what you are doing, and if you're doing it right, if you've never done it before? Also keep a log of feeds, pees and poops.

But, even with the very best of care and support, unfortunately, breastfeeding can be hard in the first few days and that's just normal. Sometimes breastfeeding problems can take weeks to figure out. In the meantime, feed the baby.

I send wishes for your journey to be what you want it to be.

Bobbi Philipp, MD

CHAPTER 18

What to Expect:
The First Few Days

Weight

BABIES ARE BORN WITH an abundance of fluid, so almost all newborns lose weight during their first few days of life, whether breastfed or formula-fed. This is normal. The exclusively breastfed infant may lose up to 10% of their birth weight. When mom's milk fully comes in, on days 2-4, the baby begins to regain weight. Ideally, infants should return to birth weight by 7-10 days of life. Breastfed babies gain weight rapidly once mother's milk arrives, often ½-1 ounce per day (or about six ounces a week).

One factor to be aware of is how much IV fluid the mother received during labor. Too much may be why babies born by Cesarean section are known to lose more weight than babies born by vaginal deliveries. Once the baby is born, ask for a 24-hour weight and use that as the starting point for the baby's weight loss. This will reflect more of a true birth weight, with the IV fluids flushed out of the baby's system.

Colostrum

The mammary glands produce colostrum, the first milk, towards the end of the pregnancy and then for several days after the baby is born. This first milk is important milk because babies are born with immature immune systems placing them at high risk for infection. Colostrum provides infection protection.

Ten Cool Facts about Colostrum

- Colostrum is a thick, yellow, sticky fluid.
- Colostrum is concentrated nutrition. Mothers make about 3 tablespoons of colostrum on the first day of the baby's life and 13 tablespoons on the second day. These are perfect amounts for the size of the baby's stomach each day. The amount increases with each feed.
- Colostrum is high in protein and low in fat, which make it easy to digest.
- Colostrum offers maximum protection against infection, perfect for the newborn whose immune system is immature.
- Colostrum is high in an immunoglobulin called secretory IgA. The newborn's intestinal cells are permeable (leaky) early on. Secretory IgA acts like a protective spray lining the baby's gut, not allowing any bad bacteria or germs to get into the baby's blood stream.
- Colostrum is high in white blood cells that are alive: macrophages, neutrophils and lymphocytes. Each type of cell has a special job. For example, macrophages hunt for germs in the baby's gut and gobble them up.
- Colostrum contains high levels of lactoferrin, an iron-binding protein. Two bacteria that are particularly dangerous to newborns, staph and E. Coli, need iron. Lactoferrin deprives these bacteria of iron.
- Colostrum facilitates the establishment of bifidus flora (good bacteria) in the baby's digestive tract. Colostrum also contains high levels of oligosaccharides, the food for the good bacteria. Are you seeing that this is the perfect system?
- Colostrum is high in fat-soluble vitamin A.
- Colostrum has a laxative effect which helps pass meconium, which aids in keeping the bilirubin level down.

Time to make the milk

The mother's milk-producing system is primed during pregnancy. The full "GO" signal occurs when the entire placenta is passed after the baby is born. Then, when the baby suckles at the breast and stimulates the nipple-areolar area, more "go" signals are sent to the pituitary gland in the brain to release two hormones, prolactin and oxytocin. Prolactin is responsible for milk production; oxytocin is responsible for the let down of milk. Oxytocin is also known as the "love" or "bonding" hormone. Try to hold your baby as much as possible in skin-to-skin contact in the first 24 hours. Putting the baby to breast frequently signals the mother's brain and body to make milk and allows the full milk supply to arrive as soon as possible.

Move the Milk Early and Often

In addition to prolactin and oxytocin, two other factors influence milk production. Lactation Inhibition Factor (LIF) is a substance found in milk. If milk sits in the breast and LIF accumulates, that may signal the system to shut down milk production. Thus, there is a need to empty breasts regularly or "on demand." You need to move the milk to make the milk.

The Prolactin Receptor Theory states that, in the first few weeks of life, prolactin receptors are being set up and activated. If breasts are emptied, more and more receptors are set up and activated. If breasts are full of milk, the prolactin receptors get stretched and don't work quite right and fewer are set up. In time, milk production will decrease. This explains why a formula-feeding mother can come in to a pediatrician's office at two weeks and say that she changed her mind and now she wants to breastfeed. She most likely will have a hard time with milk production, as her prolactin receptors were not set up properly in the first two weeks. When babies are fed formula, the breasts are not emptied. The bottom line is to empty the breasts, empty the breasts, empty the breasts.

The asymmetric latch

"The latch" describes the way the infant takes the breast and transfers milk into the mouth. A good latch is crucial to breast-feeding success. It prevents sore nipples in the mother (the #2 reason women quit breastfeeding), ensures sufficient milk transfer, and provides enough stimulation to the nipple/breast for plentiful, continued milk production.

The key to avoiding pain and ensuring maximum milk transfer is for the baby to take as much of the breast as possible into the mouth. In this way the nipple is protected in the back of the mouth, being pushed up against the soft palate (not the hard palate that is towards the front of the mouth). The tongue should always be below the nipple. Beware of tongue-suckers or chompers, babies who have been sucking their tongues while in utero and do the same when put to the breast.

The key is for the latch to be asymmetric. To get started, hold the breast in a "C-hold", with four fingers below and the thumb above the breast, away from the nipple, to offer maximum support of the breast, and to ensure that the fingers do not get in the infant's way during latch on. Stroking the baby's upper lip with the nipple will elicit the rooting reflex. Be patient. When the infant gapes or opens the mouth widely, whisk the baby up an over and onto the breast. Doing this encourages the infant to take a full mouthful of breast tissue, as if the baby were about to eat a Big Mac™ Sandwich. Take care that the baby doesn't just grab onto the tip of the nipple.

Remember it is breastfeeding, not nipple feeding.

A newborn can be held in many different positions to breast-feed. A favorite is called laid-back breastfeeding or biological nurturing. In this position the mother is semi reclined so all of her body is supported and relaxed. The baby's body is supported tummy to mummy! The baby recreates the first breast crawl and comes up and over the nipple/areolar complex to obtain a good, deep, asymmetrical latch. Check out videos on YouTube on laid-back breastfeeding.

Other ways to hold the baby when breastfeeding include: the cradle hold, the football hold, on-the-side lying position and a laid-back position. Most women naturally use the "cradle hold", with the baby cradled in the mother's arms, facing her, so a straight line could pass from the infant's ear through the shoulder and hip. Baby and mother are positioned tummy-to-tummy, nipple to nose. To prevent a sore back, bring the baby to you, not your breast to the baby.

Babies born via cesarean-birth are often held in the "football-hold" at the mother's side with the feet tucked under her arm to avoid pressure on the mother's abdominal sutures.

For the "side-lying position", mother and infant lie together side-by-side, again, tummy-to-tummy, together in bed.

Be sure to take advantage of Quiet Time. You will need to rest during the day so you are ready for nighttime feedings. Limit visitors while you are in the hospital. Just say no. Tell them you can't wait to see them all once you are home. Use your nurse as a bodyguard to keep visitors out. Place a sign on your door that says "Do Not Disturb. See Nurse."

Maternity staff should be evaluating the latch while you are in the hospital. The American Academy of Pediatrics recommends that evaluation occur at least once every shift. At Boston Medical Center this means at least once every eight hours. Signs of a successful latch include:

- Flanged out fish lips
- A wide angle at the corner of the mouth
- More areola showing on the top than the bottom (asymmetric latch)
- Chin touching the breast
- Nose away from the breast
- No clicking sounds
- Puffed out cheeks
- Rhythmical jaw movement (suck, suck, swallow)

Watch this video on YouTube for great tips about getting a good latch.
Breastfeeding Attachment – Breastfeeding Series
May 20, 2015   Global Health Media Project   10 minutes and 18 seconds long

Hand expression

New mothers should be taught hand expression and encouraged to hand express after every breastfeed. The drops of colostrum extracted can be fed to the baby using a spoon. While it can take up to 24 hours to obtain any milk with an electric pump, with hand expression milk is produced right away. Old maternity care relied on pacifiers and bottles; new maternity care encourages skin-to-skin holding and hand expression.

Hand expression:

1. Is a great way to get colostrum
2. May work better than a pump
3. Helps the baby to attach
4. Relieves engorgement

How to hand express:

1. Sit up.
2. Stimulate your breasts by rubbing or massaging them.
3. Correctly position your hand with your thumb and forefinger in a "C" position, back behind the areola. The thumb and fingertip of the forefinger should be lined up so a straight line would pass through them with the nipple in the middle.
4. Press back against your chest. Gently roll your two fingers forward, without sliding along the skin. It may take a few minutes to get going.
5. Move your C-shaped thumb and forefinger around your press to express all quadrants or areas of the breast. Hand express on one side and then move to the other, then back and forth.

"I don't have any milk"

The #1 reason women stop breastfeeding in the hospital setting is because they think they don't have enough milk.

But the fact is, if breastfeeding is managed well, inadequate milk supply is rare. A new mother makes about 3 tablespoons of milk (~50cc) during the entire first day after birth, 13 tablespoons (~250cc) on day 2, abundant amounts when the milk "comes in" on days 2 to 4, and up to 500cc by the fifth day of the baby's life. This is just the right amount for your new infant whose stomach is only the size of his/her fist. A newborn's stomach can hold 7 cc per feed in the first 0-24 hours, 14 cc per feed from 24-48 hours, and 34 cc per feed on the third day of life.

When a 12-hour-old baby is fed 1½ ounces (45cc) of infant formula, the baby's stomach is too small to hold such a large amount of food. The overflow has to go somewhere; you may see the formula dribbling from the corners of the mouth, as well as coming out the nose. You may also see the telltale yellow stains on the baby's johnnie and bassinette cover. In addition, this overfeeding shuts down feeding cues and creates a vicious negative cycle where the baby goes to the breast less often, removes smaller and smaller amounts of breast milk, and the mother's breast produces less. While it may be comforting to know exactly how much is being taken, bottle feeds cause breastfeeding troubles. Hand expression is a great way to know that you do have milk!

HOW BIG is the baby's stomach in the first few days of life?

THIS BIG:
Day of life one – blueberry, day 2 – grape, day 4 – strawberry, day 7 – lime

How big is your new baby's stomach?
This big.

Day 1   Day 2   Day 4   Day 7

Pees and poops

A newborn should pee at least once on day one and at least twice on day two, and then more often as your milk comes in. Another way to think of it is once on day of life one and then adding one to that for each day forward up to 6. So on day of life 5, the baby would pee 5 times. Keep in mind that super absorbent diapers can make it difficult to actually tally urinations. You can also count poops (stool, bowel movements). The normal stooling sequence is:

- Day 1-2: meconium stool --- black, thick, sticky, tarry

- Day 2-4: transition stool --- darkish green, looser than meconium, like mud pie filling

- Day 3 and on: breast milk stool --- mustard-yellow and seedy, very loose, runny, often passed with every feed. A good indicator that mom's milk "is in" occurs when the color of stool changes to yellow. From day 3 on, look for 3 or more breast milk stools in 24 hours. Then, when feeding is really going well, the baby may pass a poop with every feed.

Feeding cues

Infants should be fed according to their feeding cues, not on a rigid hourly schedule. Watch the baby, not the clock. Feeding cues include:

- Hand to mouth activity
- Smacking lips
- Signs of light arousal (like closed eyes fluttering)

Crying is a late indicator of hunger in the newborn (you probably missed the early cues!)

FOR FEEDING CUES
Don't watch the clock,
Watch your baby.

Cue-based feeding ensures a good milk supply, a contented baby, and prevents engorgement (by frequently emptying the breasts).

To watch for feeding cues in the hospital, the mother needs to have her baby in the room with her, which is why rooming-in is recommended.

In the first couple of weeks of life, as breastfeeding is getting established, how often should a breastfeeding mother feed her baby?

The answer is to feed on demand. Feed frequently. The button below has a catchy saying, 8 or more in 24, but breastfeeding babies often feed more often than that. Typically, there are 11-16 feeding times within 24 hours.

How best to get breastfeeding going if a newborn is sick and has to go to the Neonatal Intensive Care Unit (NICU)? The mother should be:

1. Offered help to express her milk as soon as possible after delivery, ideally within six hours, or when the mother is medically stable and able. The sooner the better. Any colostrum produced can be taken to the NICU. Drops can be swabbed in the baby's mouth. Early expression will also maximally stimulate the mother's milk supply.

2. Advised to express her milk eight or more times in 24 hours, including at night.

3. Supported to kangaroo care her baby in the NICU.

Alternative feeding methods

If breastfeeding is not going well early on, feeding by an alternative feeding method is recommended. This serves as a bridge until the feeding at the breast improves. An alternative feeding method is basically any method of delivering the liquid that is not a bottle. It could be by a spoon, syringe, cup, dropper, finger or supplemental nursing system (SNS – discussed below). The reason for avoiding the bottle is because the suck at the bottle and the suck at the breast are different. The breastfeeding suck is a wide-open, big-angle-at-the-corner-of-the-mouth suck. The baby opens wide to get the mother's nipple placed well back in the mouth underneath the soft palate. His tongue extends beneath the breast tissue. When the baby stops sucking at the breast to swallow, the breast milk stops flowing.

The bottle nipple suck is a small-angle-at-the-corner-of-the-mouth suck. The nipple is forward in the baby's mouth up against the hard palate. The milk flows fairly readily from the nipple once an initial suction is created and then the baby simply controls the flow by placing his tongue over the hole(s) in the nipple while he swallows.

In addition, liquid flows in quickly from the bottle. These dynamics are different than when the baby drinks from the breast — the baby has to suck a bit to get the let down to occur (i.e., the liquid comes in slower), and the volume is limited.

As the sucks are quite different and a brand-new baby is just learning, this can get confusing Some babies can handle the different sucks, but some can't. Most get confused and will almost always prefer the bottle suck and the quicker flow rate.

Because bottle-feeding can make breastfeeding difficult, alternative feeding methods should be tried if there is a need to feed the baby while breastfeeding issues are being addressed. These include feeding by a: spoon, syringe, cup, dropper, finger or supplemental nursing system (SNS). A SNS is a tube attached to a syringe. The tube can be threaded into the baby's mouth when the baby is sucking on the breast, and previously expressed breast milk, donor milk or formula can be slowly dropped into the baby's mouth while breastfeeding.

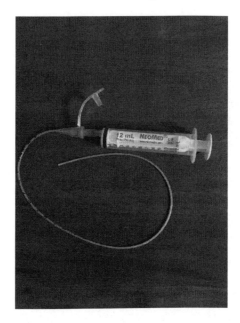

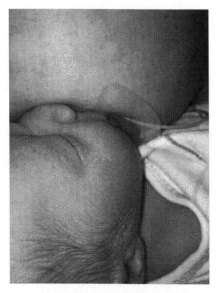

Here is my grandson, Anthony, feeding in the early days with the help of a nipple shield and a SNS device containing donor milk.

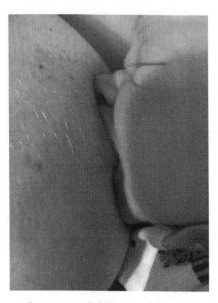

Here is Anthony about a week later at a Lactation Consultant visit. This was his latch without the nipple shield, but my daughter ended up using the shield for about two months.

We use alternative feeding methods in the hospital, but will never send a baby home using any of these methods. Many problems can be turned around quickly. Others take more time and will need to be worked on once home with the help of a lactation consultant. To go home a baby needs to be able suck/swallow at the breast or from a bottle and should be taught paced bottle feeding (see video by the Milk Mob on YouTube). Some recommend the Dr. Brown bottle with a premie nipple. In studies this has been shown to be a slow flow nipple. This nipple is laser cut so the flow rate is consistent from one Dr. Brown premie nipple to another and the slower rate mimics the flow at the breast. Others prefer a nipple that is wide based with a slow flow like a Lansinoh mOmma (with slow flow nipple) or Comotomo (with slow flow nipple). You don't want the baby to get used to the milk coming in really fast and then try to get used to the rate at the breast.

The All Day Buffet

On the second day of life, healthy breastfeeding babies often want to eat at the breast all day and night long. This is known as the "fussy day 2's" or the "All Day Buffet." Because moms are often very tired at this point, this is a difficult time. Moms should be told about this normal behavior and be encouraged to hang in there, as with each feed more and more milk will come in.

Pacifiers

Offering pacifiers to healthy breastfeeding babies in the early days of life may adversely affect breastfeeding. Time spent sucking on a pacifier is time not spent sucking at the breast. Pacifiers interfere with the baby's feeding cues and also make it more difficult for the baby to attach to the breast. The lack of stimulation and the decreased removal of milk from the breasts can delay the arrival of the full milk supply.

Volumes have been written about binkies. The AAP makes this recommendation in their 2012 Statement, Breastfeeding and the

Use of Human Milk: "Given the documentation that early use of pacifiers may be associated with less successful breastfeeding, pacifier use in the neonatal period should be limited to specific medical situations. These include for pain relief, as a calming agent, or as part of a structured program for enhancing oral motor function. Because pacifier use has been associated with a reduction in SIDS incidence, mothers of healthy term infants should be instructed to use pacifiers at infant nap or sleep time after breastfeeding is well established, at approximately 3 to 4 weeks of age."

The Boston Medical Center Pacifier Policy allows pacifiers:

1. For babies on the Neonatal Abstinence Syndrome (NAS) Policy

2. For babies in the Neonatal Intensive Care Unit (NICU)

3. For significant mother/baby separation (example: mom in the Intensive Care Unit)

4. If parents bring one in on their own (with education on the issue documented)

We used to use pacifiers during circumcisions, with the rule being that they were to be thrown out before the baby returned to the mother's room. We found this slope was too slippery, however, as sometimes pacifiers ended up in the bassinette traveling back with the baby. Now the baby sucks on a nurse's gloved finger during the procedure.

Supplementation

Sometimes supplementation is medically necessary. Reasons include issues like excessive weight loss or a high bilirubin level (hyperbilirubinemia). There is a way to supplement, that is to feed the baby but not wreck the breastfeeding. The goal of a supplemental feeding plan is to feed the baby, move the mother's milk, and keep the baby breast oriented.

Here is an example of an order to begin a Supplemental Feeding Plan:

1. Breastfeed on demand, but at least every three hours.

2. Then, supplement with expressed breast milk/donor milk/

formula to equal up to 10 ml (day or life one), up to 20 ml (day of life two), up to 30 ml (day or life three) every three hours. Use all expressed breast milk or donor milk first.

3. Offer supplements via an alternative feeding method of mother's choice (spoon, cup, syringe, supplemental nursing system/SNS, dropper).

4. Pump between breastfeeding, at least every three hours.

CHAPTER 19

Donor Milk

WHEN A MOTHER'S OWN breast milk isn't available or of adequate volume, donated milk from another mother is available from Milk Banks located across the United States. The Level III Neonatal Intensive Care Unit (NICU) at Boston Medical Center (BMC) has been using donor milk for vulnerable premature infants since June 2011. All Level III NICUs in Boston use donor milk. The BMC Mother Baby Unit began offering donor milk in December 2015. The source of donor milk used at BMC is Mothers' Milk Bank Northeast located in Newton Upper Falls, Massachusetts.

Mothers' Milk Bank Northeast is a non-profit community milk bank that operates under the guidelines of the Human Milk Banking Association of North America (HMBANA). It provides donated, pasteurized human milk to babies in Boston, Massachusetts, and throughout the Northeastern United States. HMBANA currently has 27 member banks.

How is donor milk collected and processed?

The process begins with a woman who volunteers to pump and donate her milk. HMBANA donors are not paid. Eligibility criteria of the donating mother include:

- The mother and her infant are in good health and have approval by the mother's obstetrician and infant's pediatrician.
- The mother cannot smoke or regularly use any medications, herbs or megavitamins.

- The mother cannot consume more than two ounces of hard liquor or equivalent in a 24-hour period.

The donating mother participates in a triple screening process:

1. Completion of a questionnaire and verbal phone interview with the mother
2. Completion of a questionnaire by the mother and her infant's physician stating that the mother and infant in good health
3. The mother's blood is screened and found to be negative for:
   - HIV 1, 2, 0
   - HTLV 1, 2
   - Hepatitis B and C
   - RPR (syphilis)
   (The Milk Bank pays for the cost of the blood screens)

Once approved, the mother:

- Pumps and then freezes her milk as soon as possible
- Sends her frozen milk via Fed Ex to the milk bank
- Can donate her milk for up to one year
- Has her blood screens repeated every six months

When the milk arrives at the Milk Bank it is thawed, pooled with 3-5 other donor's milk, poured into bottles, and then heat pasteurized. One bottle of each batch is opened and tested for bacteria. If any bacteria are found, the entire batch is thrown out. If no bacteria are found, the milk is refrozen and is ready to be shipped out.

Milk from donors with preterm infants are processed and stored separately from women with full term infants

Donor milk costs $4.50 per ounce, which pays for the processing and shipping costs. Donor milk comes in different sized bottle. BMC orders the 100cc size. BMC is paying for the donor milk used in the NICU out of a philanthropic fund established in honor of our past CEO, Elaine Ullian. Donor milk used in the Mother Baby Unit is paid for out of the nursing cost center.

Both units have policies in place for ordering, logging,

monitoring, warming and using donor milk. Once thawed, the bottle of milk is good for 48 hours.

One example of using donor milk on the Mother Baby Unit:

A newborn who arrived a little early at 37 weeks is 39 hours old and the screening bilirubin level is high enough to warrant starting phototherapy. The mother is exclusively breastfeeding. The most recent weight showed the baby to be down 11%. In this case we would start phototherapy and then start a supplemental feeding plan. The lactation team would be consulted to help the mother with feeds and observe latches. They would help the mother with hand expression and electric pumping. The pediatric team would order a supplemental feeding plan: put the baby to breast on feeding cues, pump after feeds but at least every three hours, feed the baby via a spoon whatever the mother pumps plus a certain amount of donor milk every three hours (if the mother consents to donor milk use). Once the mother's own milk increases and the baby's weight improves, the donor milk would be stopped.

CHAPTER **20**

Information for The Mother Who Wishes to Formula Feed

MOTHERS WHO CHOOSE TO formula feed are encouraged to safely hold their baby skin-to-skin for at least one hour after birth and then often when they are on the post-partum unit. Education includes discussing appropriate volumes per feed for each day, reviewing a paced-bottle feeding video, and feeding the baby on feeding cues. Prior to discharge, information is given and reviewed on safe formula preparation.

Preparing Powdered Formula

- Most people used powdered formula, as it is the least expensive. Your baby's doctor may recommend a specific type of formula for your baby. It is okay to use the store brand versions of name brand formulas. When buying formula, check for expiration dates.

- Start by washing your hands and the table or countertop you will be using. Bottles and nipples should be sterilized by boiling them for ten minutes after washing in the dishwasher or with hot soapy water and rinsed well. A bottlebrush is very helpful.

- Clean off the top of the can before opening. Do not store the scoop in the can after handling it.

- Follow the directions carefully. Formula made with too much or too little water could cause dehydration, diarrhea or poor growth. The American Academy of Pediatrics does not recommend mixing the powder formula with hot water. However, the World Health Organization (WHO) and Centers for Disease Control and Prevention (CDC) do recommend mixing the formula powder with hot water, 158 degrees F (70 degrees C) and above, to kill any bacteria in the powder. Powdered formula is not sterile, so by mixing it with the boiled water the risk of illness is reduced. Measure the correct amount of the heated water first, and then add the powder and mix well by gently shaking. Cool the formula before feeding by running bottles under tap water or placing in an ice bath. Check the temperature on your wrist before feeding. No matter which way you do it, the formula can be used immediately or stored in the refrigerator for up to 24 hours.

• Tap water can be used to mix formula. If you have well water talk to your baby's doctor to see if yours is safe. Nitrates found in well water can harm infants. Bottled water may be used if you have not had your water tested.

Safe Storage and Handling

• Do not heat formula in the microwave as it can result in burns to the baby's mouth. Place bottles in a small bowl filled with warm water to gently warm them over 5-10 minutes. Be sure to check the temperature before feeding. Once you begin feeding the baby, the formula must be used within one hour or thrown away.

Feeding Tips

• Feed your baby when you notice feeding cues, not on a schedule.

• Cradle the baby in your arms; holding the head higher than the tummy. Slow the feeds down. Watch a "paced bottle feeding video" on You Tube. Each time you feed, switch sides to help your baby develop strong neck muscles. Never prop the bottle or put the baby to bed with a bottle.

• Newborns have small stomachs so be careful not to overfeed as this can cause vomiting and diarrhea. Burp the baby as needed or after every ½ – 1 ounce of formula. Most newborns eat about eight times per day or every 2-4 hours.

Heading home

As you get ready to head home, here are some tips to ensure breastfeeding success:

1. The baby should be put to breast at least 8 or more times in 24 hours.

2. The baby should pass 3 or more bowel movements in 24 hours.

3. The baby should have 6 or more wet diapers in 24 hours.

4. The baby should be hungry and demanding, not sleepy and quiet.

5. You should be given information about breastfeeding support groups or a telephone support line to call when you are home.

6. A knowledgeable clinician should see the baby at 3-5 days of life to check the weight, the latch, heart, and the baby's color.

7. When you get home, hydrate – eat – and rest when you can. Take care of yourself and your baby. Let others do everything else.

CHAPTER 21

Cheat Sheet for Parents: What to Expect

- The early breast milk you make is called colostrum. Colostrum, the first milk, is nicknamed 'liquid gold' because it contains so many good things including a whooping dose of infection protection.

- Expect the first week to be hard, especially the 2nd day. After the first week, breastfeeding becomes easier. Try to take this new journey one hour, one day at a time.

- Your body is set up to make the perfect amount of breast milk. Early on, your baby's stomach is small so it cannot hold a lot of liquid all at once.

  - On day 1, you will make 3 Tablespoons of milk;
  - On day 2, you will make 13 Tablespoons of milk; and
  - Around day 3, you will make a lot of milk (when your full milk "comes in").

- Studies show a baby's stomach can hold: 7cc/feed (0-24 hrs), 14 cc/feed (24-48 hrs), 34 cc/feed (48-72 hrs). When a baby is overfed, the only place the extra liquid can go is out – through the mouth and the nose. In addition, too much food decreases feeding cues.

- Babies normally <u>lose</u> weight during the first days of life; up to 10% weight loss can be normal. Babies born by C-sections tend to lose a little more weight than babies born by vaginal births.

Baby talk for "I'm hungry" includes: 1) sucking on FISTS/FINGERS; 2) smacking lips; 3) eyes open and arms and legs moving around. When you see these signals, called feeding cues, it's time to eat! Crying may be a late indicator of hunger.

- Keep your baby right next to you, in your room, so you can watch for the feeding cues.

- THere are many diFFerent ways to hold your baby. THe classic way is to hold your baby 'tummy to tummy', 'nipple to nose', so your baby is lined up so you could pass a ruler from your baby's ear-to-shoulder-to-hip. Laid back nursing is also a good way to help the baby latch.

- THe latch is the way your baby sucks on your breast to get the milk into the stomach.

- For a good latch, tickle the middle of your baby's face with your nipple. THen wait until he/she opens the mouth as wide as possible – put as much breast as possible into the mouth.

- Ask hospital staFF to check your latch and teach you how to hand express.

- As your milk comes in your baby's bowel movements will change from thick, sticky black stools to dark brown stools to loose, somewhat chunky yellow/green stools. THe yellow/green stools are normal breastfeeding stools that indicate a lot of milk is coming in.

- Newborns do not feed on a regular schedule; they cluster feed. THey may eat and eat and eat and then rest and then eat and then rest and then eat, rest, eat... THe pattern is irregular.

- When you go home, your baby should eat at least 8-12 times in 24 hours and poop at least three times in 24 hours.

- Your pediatrician will want to see your baby at 3-5 days of life to check weight, latch, and color.

- Avoid paciFIers until breastfeeding is well established (about 3-4 weeks).

- For the FIrst month of life, if you can, avoid using a bottle. THe suck at the breast is a wide-open mouth suck; the suck on a bottle nipple is a small-mouth suck. A lot of formula comes out fast when a baby drinks from a bottle — this is not how breast milk comes from the breast. Thus, babies get confused and may not be able to do both right away. Once the baby gets breastfeeding down, he/she can always bottle feed. If you need to use a bottle, go with a slow flow nipple and pace bottle feed.

- Trust yourself. The first week is often tough, but you can do it! Ask for help.

- Breastfeeding may not go as planned and that's ok. If there are issues, FEED THE BABY. Get help. Hang in there. Keep working on it. Take it one hour at a time every day.

Chapter 22

Baby Friendly and the Code

How do you know if your maternity hospital is just ok – pretty good – or great at supporting breastfeeding? One way is to inquire if the hospital has the Baby-Friendly designation or is working to get the designation. Baby-Friendly is an international designation awarded by the World Health Organization and UNICEF that recognizes maternity hospitals for excellence in breastfeeding support. A hospital with this award follows the Ten Steps to Successful Breastfeeding, pays a Fair Market Value for formula and formula products, and is Code compliant (which is explained below).

The Ten Steps to Successful Breastfeeding, the framework of the Baby-Friendly initiative, include:

1. Have a written breastfeeding policy that is routinely communicated to all health care staff.

2. Train all health care staff in skills necessary to implement this policy.

3. Inform all pregnant women about the benefits and management of breastfeeding.

4. Help mothers initiate breastfeeding within one hour of birth.

5. Show mothers how to breastfeed and how to maintain lactation even if they should be separated from their infants.

6. Give newborn infants no food or drink other than breast milk unless medically indicated.

7. Practice rooming-in: allow mothers and infants to remain together-24 hours a day.

8. Encourage breastfeeding on demand.

9. Give no artificial teats or pacifiers (also called dummies or soothers) to breastfeeding infants.

10. Foster the establishment of breastfeeding support groups and refer mothers to them on discharge from the hospital or clinic.

For example, Step 3 means that mothers who are receiving prenatal care at the hospital are given information on what to expect (like rooming in and skin to skin holding) and information on the management of breastfeeding. To meet the prenatal education requirements, we created a video in 4 languages. Mothers are asked to hold their smart phone over the QRc code of the appropriate language below and a 6-minute video pops up.

A Baby-Friendly hospital is compliant with the Code, which is short for the International Code of Marketing of Breast Milk Substitutes. The Code is a set of guidelines regarding the marketing of infant formula and formula products in the hospital setting.

Compliance with the Code means no:

- Formula company advertising and free samples to parents
- Formula company gifts and free samples to health professionals
- Posters, marketing materials and free formula gifts to health facilities
- Promotion of unsuitable products for babies (such as sweetened condensed milk)

A Baby-Friendly hospital pays fair market value for formula and formula products, no longer getting them for free from the formula industry.

Approximately 20,000 hospitals have received the Baby-Friendly award worldwide. In Sweden, every hospital is a Baby-Friendly hospital; in New Zealand 96% of the hospitals have the designation. In the United States, as of March, 2019 over a million babies are being born each year in over 500 Baby-Friendly designated facilities, representing 27% of births per year (up from 2.9% in 2007). This represents about 17% of the facilities, as there are approximately 3000 maternity facilities in the United States. The increase has been aided by Centers for Disease Control (CDC)-funded initiatives like Best Fed Beginnings and EMPower Breastfeeding. The W. K. Kellogg Foundation is funding other projects including the MotherBaby Summit Initiative and CHAMPS. These projects help hospitals get to the Baby-Friendly award in a step-by-step process.

Each country has an organization that is responsible for the Baby-Friendly Initiative, with all countries following the rules set by the World Health Organization. In the United States, the group is Baby-Friendly USA. Hospitals working on the Baby-Friendly designation enter into Baby-Friendly USA's 4D Pathway: D1-Discovery, D2-Development, D3 – Dissemination, D4-Designation.

- D1 – Discovery: the hospital contacts Baby-friendly USA about their interest, demographic information about the hospital is provided and the CEO of the hospital signs a statement that the hospital is aware they will need to pay fair-market value for formula and formula products.

- D2 – Development: a task force is formed, the hospital feeding policy is written, plans are made for staFF education and prenatal education, and data collection is started likes rates of rooming in and skin to skin holding.

- D3 – Dissemination: plans are implemented, data are obtained

- D4 – Designation: the hospital prepares for a two-day site visit by Baby-Friendly assessors.

Studies show that both overall breastfeeding and exclusive breastfeeding increase in hospitals designated as Baby-Friendly.

Philipp BL, Merewood A, Miller LW, et al. The Baby-Friendly Hospital Initiative improves breastfeeding initiation rates in a US hospital setting. *Pediatrics.* 2001;108(3):677-681.

- The authors studied breastfeeding rates at Boston Medical Center, an inner-city safety net hospital, over a four-year period from 1995 to1999. The hospital received the Baby-Friendly designation in 1999.

- Any amount of breastfeeding increased from 58% to 86.5%.

- Exclusive breastfeeding in the hospital setting prior to discharge increased from 5.5% to 33.5% (statistically significant at P=<.001).

Lancet Breastfeeding Series Group
Rollins NC, Bhandari N, Hajeebhoy N, et al. Lancet Breastfeeding Series Group. Why invest, and what it will take to improve breastfeeding practices? *Lancet.* 2016;387(10017):491-504.

- Meta-analysis of studies analyzing implementation of the BFHI

- Any breastfeeding increased by 66% (95% Confidence Interval, 34%-107%)

- Exclusive breastfeeding increased by 49% (95% Confidence Interval, 33%-68%)

Best Fed Beginnings (CDC-Funded project to help 90 hospitals achieve Baby-Friendly award)
Feldman-Winter L, Ustianov J, Anastasio J, et al. Best Fed

Beginnings: A nationwide quality improvement initiative to increase breastfeeding. *Pediatrics*. 2017;140(1):e20163121.

- Overall breastfeeding increased from 79% to 83% (t=1.93; P=.057)
- Exclusive breastfeeding increased from 39% to 61% (t=9.72; P=<.001)

Merewood A, Bugg K, Burnham L, et al. Addressing racial inequities in breastfeeding in the southern United States. *Pediatrics*. 2019; 143(2):e20181897.

- This paper links successful implementation of Baby-Friendly practices in the southern U.S. with increases in breastfeeding rates and improved, evidence-based care. The changes were especially positive for African-American women.

- Between 2014 and 2017, 33 hospitals enrolled into the Communities and Hospitals Advancing Maternity Practices (CHAMPS) program. All birthing hospitals in Greater New Orleans, and 18 in Mississippi, signed up. Over the 3 years of the project, breastfeeding initiation at CHAMPS hospitals rose from 66% to 75%, and, among African Americans, from 43% to 63%. The gap between White and Black breastfeeding rates decreased by 9.6%.

Chapter 23

Special Situations and Common Challenges

23a Early Bloomers – The Late Preterm Infant

The definition of late preterm is an infant born between 34.0 and 36.6 weeks.

Every maternity unit has a policy that clarifies where the baby is admitted after birth. At Boston Medical Center (BMC), all infants born before 35 weeks go to the Neonatal Intensive Care Unit (NICU) so they can be watched closely. An infant born between 35.0-35.6 weeks is admitted to the NICU for 12-24 hours. If the baby does well, she can then be transferred to the Mother Baby Unit to room in with the mother. A healthy infant born at 36 weeks or older is admitted with the mother to her room on the Mother Baby Unit.

A late preterm infant requires careful attention. The infant is at a higher risk of low temperature (hypothermia), low blood sugar (hypoglycemia), high bilirubin levels (hyperbilirubinemia), and infection (sepsis). They also need careful feeding plans, because they are almost always pokey eaters.

The Early Bloomer program at BMC provides exceptional care for late preterm infants admitted to the Mother Baby Unit. Upon arrival:

- The mother receives a bag containing an Early Bloomers Parent Guide, an Early Bloomers sign to hang on the bassinette, a colostrum spoon, a QRc code that links to a hand expression video, and a special hat.
- Frequent safe skin-to-skin holding is encouraged.
- Hand expression is encouraged and supported after every feeding. If the newborn is not feeding effectively, pumping is initiated at 6 hours of life to achieve adequate supply.

Admission orders are entered using a special late preterm order set:

- Vital signs every 4 hours for 48 hours, then every 8 hours.
- Reason to notify the MD: Temperature remains below 97.7° or above 99.3°
- Blood sugar levels per unit protocol – once in the first hour of life and then three pre-feed checks. If the feeding is dysfunctional after that, check blood sugars at 24 and 48 hours, or sooner if baby showing signs of hypoglycemia.
- Delay the bath for a minimum of 24 hours. Delay the bath an additional 12 hours if the baby is feeding poorly, their blood sugar is less than 50, or their temperature is less than 97.7°.
- Circumcision for males babies should be delayed 24-36 hours or longer if he is feeding poorly.
- Lactation consult
- Swallowing consult
- Eligible for donor milk
- Hold a team huddle (Mother, RN, MD/NP) every 12 hours if problems arise.

A supplemental feeding plan was discussed in a previous section and would be used for an Early Bloomer if feeding problems persist:
Breastfeed on demand; but at least every three hours. Then supplement with previously expressed breast milk/donor milk/formula to equal up to 10 ml (Day of Life 1), up to 20 ml (DOL 2), up to 30 ml (DOL 3) every three hours. Use all expressed

breast milk first. Offer supplements via an alternative feeding method of mother's choice (spoon, cup, syringe, dropper, SNS). Pump between breastfeeding; but at least every three hours.

23b Engorgement

While you are in the hospital you most likely will have plenty of help and little milk. Once home, in the epitome of bad timing, the situation reverses and you will have plenty of milk and little help. When your milk "comes in" you may become engorged when there is so much milk that breasts become full and firm and the nipples are hard for the baby to find and latch on to. A crying infant and an engorged mom are not a good match. If your baby is unable to latch because the nipple is lost in a tense, firm breast, manually express as much milk from the breast as possible until the baby becomes able to latch. Milk will drip or flow from your breasts if you stand in a shower with warm water flowing over the breasts. You can also lean over and submerge both breasts into a sink or a dishpan filled with warm water, allowing gravity and warmth to drain milk from the breasts. With the breasts and areolas softened, it will become easier for the baby to latch on. The baby is an engorged mother's best friend because the more milk that is removed from the breast the better you will feel. Putting the baby to the breast often will ease the engorgement. If the pain is intense, take acetaminophen (Tylenol) or ibuprofen (Advil or Motrin). Both categories of drug are fine to take while breastfeeding. After expressing as much milk out of your breasts as possible, reduce blood flow to the breasts by applying ice packs (frozen bags of vegetables are the ideal size). With time, your body will adjust the amount of milk made to your baby's needs, and the engorgement will cease.

23c Inverted Nipples

Nipples come in different sizes and shapes. They may be everted, short, flat, or inverted. The everted nipple, which sticks out when rubbed or stimulated, is the easiest for the infant to latch onto. Many women have flat nipples, which will become erect when stimulated, or which the infant can pull out once the breast is inside the mouth. However, true inverted nipples retract into the breast rather than stand out when pressure is put on the areola or when the nipple is rubbed or stimulated.

Although flat nipples are sometimes difficult for the baby to latch onto, most babies eventually manage to pull out a flat nipple. If you have true inverted nipples, it can be tough for the baby to achieve a good latch. You may have to use an electric breast pump to pull the nipple out as far as possible, and you may need to pump for extra stimulation and offer supplemental milk if your baby is unable to obtain enough from the breast. Studies have shown that prenatal manipulation of the nipples using breast shells or 'Hoffman's exercises' as sometimes recommended, do not actually work. A nipple shield could help.

23d Latch Troubles

Most infants sleep for long stretches during the first 12-14 hours after birth. However, some infants, especially infants born slightly ahead of their due date, have trouble latching onto the breast, or are sleepy beyond the first 12-14 hours, and only latch on briefly before falling asleep. If this happens, continue to offer the breast, and if the infant does not nurse well, a blood sugar level can be checked periodically. If by day two of life the infant is still sleepy or not latching, you should watch the infant closely for feeding cues, completely avoid pacifiers, and try to feed frequently whenever the infant wakes up. Try these tips to rouse a sleepy newborn: tickle the feet, wipe the face with a cool cloth, undress the baby, lie the baby down in an open space away from the parents, feed in an upright position like the football hold.

Other infants are wide-awake, but fuss and will not latch either. Calming techniques such as putting the infant skin-to-skin, offering a finger to suck before switching to the breast, and expressing colostrum onto the nipple may also give the infant additional motivation to begin eating.

If, despite all these efforts, the baby will still not latch, you should begin to hand express often and pump every three hours for about 10-15 minutes with a double set up electric breast pump in order to stimulate the milk supply. With hand expression you should get some drops, but you may not get very much milk with the electric pump. Anything you collect can be given to the infant. Both hand expression and stimulation with the pump will help establish your milk supply. Supplemental feeds, if necessary due to excessive weight loss, low blood sugar or high bilirubin levels, can be expressed milk, donor milk and/or formula and should be offered by spoon, cup, syringe, or any method other than a bottle nipple.

How to safely manage a medical problem and end up breastfeeding

We use a supplemental feeding plan to bridge a gap – when we need to feed the baby more to help a medical problem but we don't want to wreck breastfeeding in the process. The baby feeds on demand to remember the breastfeeding suck and the smell and feel of the breast. In this case we do impose time limits, recommending waking the baby up to feed at least every three hours. Mom hand expresses often and pumps every 2-3 hours for 15 minutes a time. This further stimulates the system to make milk and removes milk from the breasts. The baby is then fed either expressed breast milk or donor milk or formula every three hours. The amount and the mode of feeding are picked to not wreck the system. Feed the supplement by spoon, cup, or syringe (or by bottle if the lactation team makes that recommendation. They will provide a special bottle called "wide based, slow flow bottles" that stimulate the suck at the breast.)

23e Medications and Breastfeeding

Breastfeeding mothers often ask, "Is it ok to breastfeed if I am taking XXX medication?" The answer is determined by looking at factors that govern drug transfer across membranes into breast milk as well as the metabolism of the drug in mother and infant. These are called pharmacokinetic factors. Some are: molecular weight, protein binding and oral bioavailability.

Examples:

- Molecular weight: insulin and breastfeeding are fine because the molecular weight (size) of insulin is about 6,000 Daltons. A drug needs to be less than 800 Daltons to get into the mammary gland breast milk space. Insulin is so big it simply cannot get into the space.
- Protein binding: Diazepam (valium) is 99% protein bound so is not going to get into the breast milk space at any concerning level.
- Oral bioavailability: Heparin is destroyed in the stomach.

In most cases it is ok to breastfeed.

Two excellent resources to answer the question are:

1. LactMed (on the internet). A free app is available to download on your phone.
2. Medications and Mothers' Milk by Thomas Hale. Dr. Hale assigns a Lactation Risk Category to each medication (L1 to L5) that makes this resource a go to for the busy clinician.

23f Sore nipples

Breastfeeding should not be a painful event. During the first week there may be a little discomfort when the baby initially latches on, but this should decrease with time. If you have persistent, severe pain when the baby goes to breast, *there is a problem*. Almost always the problem is poor positioning or a poor latch so the solution is to assess and adjust the position and the latch. Sometimes that is easier said than done. Tender nipples can be treated by exposing them to air, as well as by applying breast milk and/or lanolin cream. Lansinoh™ is a commonly used brand of lanolin cream. Another favorite is Medihoney. Both function as an aid to get you through the worst of the discomfort, however, the positioning or latch will need to be fixed to solve the underlying cause. Another cause of sore nipples when the baby is older is a yeast infection ("thrush"). Think of thrush if you feel a burning sensation at the breast, and nipple soreness that develops later on in the breastfeeding course, usually not the first week. If thrush is the culprit, both you and baby should be seen by a clinician and treated with an anti-fungal agent.

23g Tongue Tie (ankyloglossia)

Head over to a mirror and look inside you mouth, under your tongue. You will see a piece of tissue that looks like a string connecting the underside of your tongue with the floor of the mouth. This is a normal piece of anatomy called the lingual frenulum.

As a baby develops inside the uterus, the tongue is fused to the floor of the mouth, but, prior to birth, some tissue (but not all) disintegrates allowing the tongue to lift up and extend forward (past the little gum pad, where the teeth will eventually come in). Sometimes too much tissue remains. This occurs in about 5% of newborns, is more common in boys than girls (2:5 to 1) and has a strong family history (21%). One typing system assigns a Type to where the insertion of the abnormal tissue is on the tongue and on the floor of the mouth. Type 1 – the lingual frenulum is abnormal and extends to the tip of the tongue and forward on the floor of the mouth, Type 2 – similar to one but the attachment on the tongue is a little farther back than the tip. In both Types 1 and 2 – when the baby tries to extend the tongue, it looks heart-shaped. For Type 3, the attachment is a bit farther back on the tongue and on the floor of the mouth, the sides of the tongue lift up, but not the middle, so the tongue has a classic cupping appearance. Rather than heart-shaped, it is more like a squared off shovel blade. Type 4 is called a posterior tongue-tie and is quite far back. Almost touching the back of the tongue and looking fibrotic (like a white string).

Sometimes tongue-ties cause a problem with breastfeeding, other times they do not. If you are having trouble with the latch, check your baby out for a tongue-tie. If you see one, give your baby's doctor a call to discuss. Getting it clipped might help.

Chapter 24

Contraindications to Breastfeeding

ACCORDING TO A 2012 statement from the American Academy of Pediatrics entitled, Breastfeeding and the Use of Human Milk, the contraindications to breastfeeding are if the mother is/has:

- HIV positive

- Using illicit drugs (ex: heroin, cocaine)

- Taking certain medications. Although most prescribed and over-the-counter drugs are safe for the breastfeeding infant, some medications may make it necessary to interrupt breast-feeding. These include radioactive isotopes, antimetabolites, cancer chemotherapy and a small number of other med-ications. The reference used at BMC is *Medications and Mothers' Milk* by Thomas Hale.

- Human T-cell leukemia virus type I or II

- Untreated brucellosis

- Active, untreated tuberculosis (separate dyad until mother is no longer infectious, expressed breast milk ok to use)

- Active herpes simplex lesions on breast (separate dyad until mother is no longer infectious, expressed milk ok to use)

- Developed varicella five days before through two days after delivery (separate dyad, expressed milk ok to use)

- Or an infant with galactosemia

Section 3

Supporting Breastfeeding
in the First Year

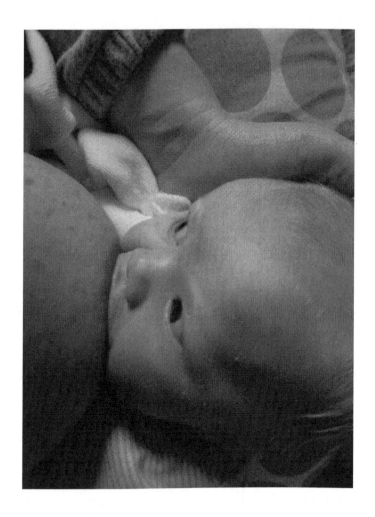

CHAPTER 25

Supporting Breastfeeding in the First Year: Twelve Tips

To review

- The goal is to breastfeed for a year.
- After discharge from the hospital, an experienced clinician should see the newborn at 3 to 5 days of life.
- The breastfeeding baby should ideally return to birth weight by 7-10 days of life.
- Normal weight gain for the breastfeeding baby is 6 ounces a week. The average breastfed baby doubles the birth weight by 4 months, and triples the birth weight by a year.
- During the first month of life, infant feeding can remain irregular – that is, cluster feeding is common. The goal remains 8 or more feeds in 24 hours.
- The AAP recommends starting a pacifier at nap time and bedtime when breastfeeding is established at 3-4 weeks of life. Both breastfeeding and pacifiers are protective against Sudden Infant Death Syndrome (SIDS).
- Practice safe sleep: place the baby back to sleep in a bare crib, breastfeed, start a pacifier once breastfeeding is established, and don't over-bundle with blankets.

Twelve tips for the first months:

1. Does the breastfeeding baby need anything else?

A. The American Academy of Pediatrics recommends that breast-feeding babies be placed on Vitamin D supplements (400 IU per day). Some pediatricians give Tri Vi Sol (Vitamins A, C and D) or Poly Vi Sol Drops (Vitamins A, C and D and other stuff) but all the baby needs is Vitamin D and a lot of babies gag on the taste and amount in the dropper. Therefore, I like Baby D Drops. It is just vitamin D and the daily dose is one drop a day. The drop can be sucked off a finger or the nipple. (Another option is for the mother to take 6400 IU of Vitamin D a day and if she does that all the baby needs to do is breastfeed.)

2. When is the best time to start a bottle?

A. Start a bottle at around 3-4 weeks. Don't wait longer than that or you risk bottle refusal. If you can, have someone else besides the mother feed the baby the bottle a day. Ideally the bottle will contain expressed breast milk.

3. What is the best bottle and nipple to use?

A. There are a lot of bottles and nipples to choose from but the main goal is to use a slow flow nipple. Here is my review of some of the popular brands.

- Dr. Brown nipples are a favorite because the premie size and Level 1 nipple have been studied and are truly slow flow. Also, the nipples are laser cut, so they are consistently the same. The downside to the Dr. Brown bottle is it has an air vent system that makes for more items to wash and, while the nipple is slow flow, it is not wide based.

- Many like the Comotomo bottle and nipple. The nipple is wide based and the bottle is soft silicone like the breast.

- My daughter used the Lansinoh mOmma bottle with a slow flow nipple as it was recommended the Lactation Consultant she saw. I was one of the primary bottle feeders and I liked this brand. The nipple is wide based so it helped my grandson to open up his mouth widely and get the big angle at the corner of his lips that we were after when he breastfed. I don't know of any studies that evaluated the flow rate of this nipple but good paced-feeding kept the flow slow.

- Many like the Kiinde brand. This system allows you to pump into twist pouches and then directly feed using the pouch so there is no transfer.

- Avent is another brand that has a wide based, slow flow nipple. For whatever bottle you use be sure to get the slow flow nipple (and the 4 – or 5-ounce size is what to purchase).

4. How much breast milk to feed?

A. A mother's normal supply is 24-30 ounces in 24 hours. Milk intake is steady from 1-6 months and then starts to decrease as the baby starts solids at around 6 months. From 9-12 months the supply is 16-18 ounces a day. After the first week and before a month of age, the baby will drink about 2 ounces a feed. A breastfeeding baby older than one month of age takes 3-4 ounces per feed. A rule of thumb to follow: feed the baby 1-1.25 ounces per hour that the mother is away (for example, if the mother is away three hours, feed the baby 3-3.75 oz.). No matter what age, usually breastfed babies don't drink more than 4 ounces per feed. Once food is started, always breastfeed first. Remember, food before one is just for fun.

5. Use paced-feeding with the bottle. This is really important. Paced bottle feeding slows the feeding down with the goal being to mimic a feeding at the breast.

- Have the feeder hold the baby away from his/her body in a semi-upright or upright position.

- Tap the baby's lips with the bottle and wait for the baby to widely open the mouth.

- Wait until the baby takes in a fair portion of the nipple, so the lips are at the base and not on the shaft or tip of the nipple.

- During feeding, hold the bottle almost horizontal so the flow isn't too fast.
- During feeding, pause the flow by lowering the bottle so there is no milk in the nipple.
- Keep repeating this. Half way through take a break and switch sides.
- Stop when the baby is done, even if there is more milk in the bottle.
- Burp the baby.
- It should take 20-30 minutes to give a bottle so the baby has time to know he is full.

Videos are available on You Tube if you search "paced bottle feeding." The Milk Mob also has a great video. Every bottle feeder for your baby needs to watch the video.

6. How do you clean the bottles and pump parts?

A. Simply rinse fairly soon after the feed and then at some point use soap and water to clean and then air dry. Another option is to use the dishwasher but you don't need to do both. No sterilization is needed. Remember that babies need exposure to germs to develop a healthy immune system. You will find you worry less about this with each child you have.

7. What foods help keep mom's milk supply up?

A. In addition to drinking a lot of water throughout the day, my daughter would eat a large bowl of oatmeal every morning, drink a Guinness beer a day, and take moringa capsules (two in the morning and two in the evening). Other ideas are Gatorade, Starbucks Pink Drink (large, no ice), lactation cookies (see recipes below) and other types of carbohydrates. If your milk supply dips, try some power pumping as shown in this graphic from www.loveandbreastmilk.com.

8. Is it ok to for a breastfeeding mother to drink alcohol?

A. The thinking on this has changed over the years. The answer is yes (in moderation of course). Because alcohol has a small molecular weight it can get into the breast milk compartment but pharmacokinetic data reveal that alcohol exits the breast milk at the same rate the alcohol exits the bloodstream. An hour after three strong drinks, your breast milk alcohol content is equivalent to a 0.07498 proof beverage. This is the equivalent of one 80 proof shot of vodka poured into 26 liters of water. This amount of alcohol content is unlikely to cause any adverse side effects in your baby. From www.kellymom. com: "In general, if you are sober enough to drive, you are sober enough to breastfeed."

9. Breastfeeding babies go through growth spurts. Feeding may be going fine and then all of a sudden, the baby wants to feed all the time. Think of this as the baby placing an order for more milk. Growth spurts tend to last 3-4 days or until the milk supply equilibrates up. A example of a classic growth spurt time is 6-8 weeks.

10. What if mom needs to stop nursing for some reason and decrease her milk supply? Try Sudafed or peppermint (like peppermint patties).

11. Regarding breastfeeding in public, the law in every state in the United States of America is that wherever you can go in public you can breastfeed. No baby should be made to eat in a bathroom stall. Period. You can cover up or you can #dropthecover. This is your right and your call.

12. Helpful websites
    • www.kellymom.com
    • www.firstdroplets.com

Chapter 26

Breast Milk Storage

Breast milk can be stored in:

Room temperature for	6-8 hours
Refrigerator for	6-8 days
Freezer for	a year
Deep freezer	a year or longer

Smell the milk before using. If it smells ok, use it.

Infant Formula (for the sake of comparison)

- Formula comes with an expiration date on the label or the bottom of the can.
- Formula should be discarded within one hour of when the baby starts to drink the bottle.
- Once opened (but not fed to the baby), ready-to-feed and concentrate liquid formulas are safe in the refrigerator for 48 hours.
- Prepared powder formula is safe in the refrigerator for 24 hours.

Fresh Breast Milk

- Freshly pumped milk is safe to sit out in room temperature for 6-8 hours.
- Breast milk in the refrigerator is good for 6-8 days.
- Extra pumped milk can be frozen at any time. Some say to consider freezing extra milk on day three as that seems to be when the bacterial count in the milk is the lowest.

- It is fine to mix freshly pumped milk with cold, older milk that is in the fridge.
- It is not recommended to add warm milk to frozen milk.
- Just like you do with a carton of cow's milk before drinking, smell the breast milk that is in the fridge before using. Spoiled milk smells and tastes foul.

This mason jar contains freshly pumped breast milk.

Extra Milk

- Use a Haaka or Milkie cups to collect dripping milk on the opposite breast.
- Combine any extra you get over 24 hours in the fridge. Some use a mason jar for storage.
- Fresh milk is the best! Remember that your freshly pumped milk can be good for up to 8 days in the fridge. As they say, don't feed the freezer. Get out of the pump, freeze, defrost cycle as that is so much extra work. When you return to work, what you pump can be refrigerated and fed to the baby the next day.
- If you plan on freezing, pour the milk into milk storage bags when you are ready, label and put in the freezer. Freezing the bag flat makes for easier stacking.

Using Breast Milk from the Fridge

- No rule says you have to warm expressed breast milk that comes out of the refrigerator. Breast milk can be given directly from the fridge – or can be given at room temperature – or can be warmed by placing it in lukewarm water (at most 40°C) over a period of about twenty minutes.

- When a baby feeds directly from the breast, obviously the milk will be warm – that is – at body temperature. Thus, when initially introducing a bottle of refrigerated milk, warming the milk may help the baby adjust.

- Colder milk may have clumps of fat floating in it. Light warming and stirring will help incorporate some of that awesome fat back into the milk.

- Some babies just have a preferred temperature. You will see!

Frozen Breast Milk

- Pumped milk can be stored in a freezer for up to a year.

- If the freezer is cold enough to freeze ice cream, it is cold enough to freeze breast milk.

- A lot of options exist for what to use for storage of your breast milk. Disposable storage bags tend to be less expensive and take up less space compared to a hard-sided container – but it's your choice. Regarding freezer bags – a lot of brands are available – Lansinoh, Target, Medela, or others like Kiinde. The Kiinde option allows you to pump directly into the bag, no need for transfer.

- Freeze breast milk in small amounts (2-4 ounces). Smaller volumes will thaw faster and less will be wasted if the baby is unable to finish all the milk.

- Using storage bags allows you to freeze it flat (see picture at bottom of this section) which makes it easier to stack. Then place the bags in something like a plastic bin or a cardboard seltzer bottle container so they won't break open when frozen and scraped. Squeeze almost all the air out of the bag before freezing, leave a small space at the top. Breast milk, like most liquids, expands when it freezes. The less air in with the milk means a smaller chance of freezer burn.

- Label the bag or container with the collection date and the amount. Also write the baby's name if a daycare provider or other caregiver will be preparing feeds.

- Choose the coldest location in the freezer to store breast milk; the back of the freezer is colder than any space near the front or in the door.

- Milk can be stored in a deep freezer for a year or more. It is probably good for a longer period of time, but since many studies end at a year, we don't really know. So freeze for whatever, defrost it, smell it, and if it smells ok – use it. Never throw out breast milk!

- Maybe you can come up with a system where you place the newest milk in the back of the freezer and the oldest milk moves to the front of the pile?

- It is ok to refreeze partially thawed frozen milk as long as ice crystals remain.

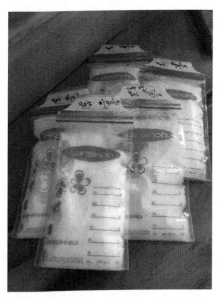

Jess pumped during work and transported the milk in a mason

jar. When she arrived "home" she transferred the milk into storage bags in 4-ounce amounts and labelled the bags. Anthony was 5 months old so he drank 4 ounces a time the next day from the Nanny or Nana (me!). Normally she would not freeze this as it would be used the next day, but in this case, we were off to another state for a vacation so we froze it.

4 oz of pumped breast milk. Lay the bag flat, press the air out, then zip. This is how we froze it flat in the freezer (of course!).

Thawing Frozen Breast Milk

- Frozen breast milk can be thawed in several ways. Frozen milk placed in a refrigerator will thaw overnight. Placing it is a container of tepid water or running it under warm tap water will speed up the thawing process and also warm it up. If you have a waterless milk warmer – lucky you! Use that.

- Do not microwave breast milk because it heats up unevenly and may cause a burn. Also microwaving significantly decreases the action of immunologic factors, which will decrease health benefits.

- The fat in breast milk rises to the top during storage so it may appear layered. Swirl or shake the milk to mix it before feeding. Breast milk may acquire tinges of color depending on the mother's diet, but it remains perfectly good to use.

- Sometimes defrosted breast milk might smell soapy or fishy or have a metallic taste. This is thought to be due to mothers with high lipase – an enzyme that mediates triglyceride (fat) breakdown releasing fatty acids. The odor is likely from the oxidation of the fatty acids. Try feeding it, as it is safe to feed and maybe the baby won't mind. If the baby is refusing it, you could put a drop of vanilla into it to see if that will mask the smell/taste. If the baby is outright refusing it, next round, try scalding the milk. Express your milk. Then heat it up to the point that bubbles are seen around the edge of the pan, but stop before it reaches the point of boiling. Then cool and freeze it.

Daycare

- Many daycare centers follow formula rules, like dumping breast milk after one hour. Yikes! These rules can be hard to fight. For this reason, plan for smaller, more frequent amounts to avoid leftovers that could get tossed.

- If the daycare center is being persnickety, ask your pediatrician to write a letter approving use of breast milk rules for the breast milk you are sending.

- Some daycare centers will put leftovers back in the fridge (awesome) so you can see how much the baby drank (fine) and then you can take it home (awesome) and you can put it into the fridge and reuse it for the next feed or next day (awesome). Before you use it, sniff or taste it. Remember, spoiled milk smells or tastes foul.

Stay at home dad/Sitter/Grandma/Nanny

- Fresh milk is best and lasts for 6-8 days in the refrigerator. Try to get out of the pump, freeze, and defrost cycle.

- Let's say the baby drinks part of never frozen, warmed milk – or milk taken out of the fridge. That bottle can sit at room temperature and be reused for up to 4-6 hours.

Again, smell it or taste it and if ok, use it.

Cleaning

- Containers and feeding devices can be rinsed and then cleaned with soap and water, air-dried or dried with a paper towel. They do not need to be sterilized.

Common Sense

- Pumping is hard work, and a time commitment. Use common sense to answer all the questions that come up. Remember that human milk is rugged. You can shake it, swirl it, freeze it, twirl it – without damaging anything. A few extra days in the fridge or a few extra months in the freezer probably are fine. Follow the mantra, "Never throw out breast milk." If it smells ok or tastes ok, use it.

Information from:

- ABM Clinical Protocol #8: Human Milk Storage Information for Home Use for Full-Term Infants, Revised 2017. Authors: Anne Eglash, Liliana Simon and The Academy of Breastfeeding Medicine.

- Dr. Milk Facebook group file on storage written by Dr. Chandria Lynn Johnson.

- Dr. Milk Facebook group posts.

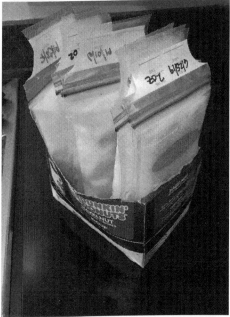

Freezing the breast milk bag flat makes for easier storage.

Chapter 26a

Tip of the Day

I CALL THESE BREAST milk pops. They are great for just fun, great for hot days, great for teething.

- Here is how to make breast milk pops:
- Pour expressed breast milk into an ice cube tray.
- Freeze.
- Buy mesh feeding bags.
- Put a frozen breast milk cube into mesh bag.
- Feed to baby (baby will suck on the mesh bag).

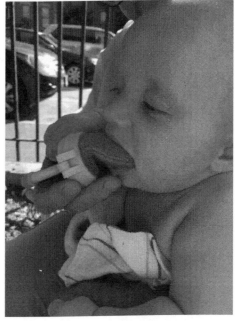

CHAPTER 27

Back to Work

Meet to Plan

PRIOR TO YOUR ACTUAL start date, meet with your boss or supervisor or HR person to discuss pumping when you return to work

- Set aside time in your day for pumping breaks (for a typical 8-hour day you might pump two or three times)
- Determine the location of a pumping room: electrical outlet, privacy, sink, fridge.

After you pump you do not need to wash all "the stuff" each time. You can put it in a zip lock bag (and then a paper bag if people are going to not like seeing it) and put it in the refrigerator, take it all home, and wash it all once with warm soapy water.

Jess pumped at work. She transported the milk home in a ma-son jar in a cooler bag. Once home she divided it up into 4 oz bottles to be used the next day. Anthony was 5 months old so was taking 4 oz at a time.

The baby needs to be fed in a way that will not consume more breast milk than you will be pumping while you are at work. What you pump at work should be put in the fridge when you get home and used for the next day's feeds. The feeding plan also needs to not discourage the baby's physical act (suck and swallow) of breastfeeding.

- Feed using paced bottle-feeding (YouTube, paced bottle feeding)

- Use a slow flow nipple.

- Feed 1-1.25 ounces for every hour you are away. For ex-ample, for each three-hour interval, the amount fed would not exceed 3-3.75 oz.

- You will need to be extremely clear with daycare providers or perhaps your mother-in-law about these volumes and paced bottle-feeding. Many people are used to amounts in the formu-la feeding culture. Formula-fed babies are often overfed. Leave bottles in the exact amount that can be used for each feed. Your freezer sash cannot be touched unless approved by you.

- Before starting solids at six months, the total over 24 hours should be 24-30 ounces.

The Freezer Stash

- You do not need to have a massive freezer stash when you head back to work because you are going to pump to feed the baby, not the freezer.

- What you pump at work goes in the fridge when you get home, and fed to the baby the next day when you are at work. If you have weekends off, the Friday pumps will be used on Monday.

- For the occasional unexpected circumstance, have three to four days-worth or a freezer stash or 90-120 ounces.

When are you going to pump?

This depends on your situation.

- Some mothers like to breast-feed their baby in the morning before they leave home. In that case, the next pumping session would be in three hours, then in three hours, then in three hours. Pumping breaks might occur at 10 am, 1 pm, and 4 pm.

- Other mothers have a long commute or need to leave the house quite early, so they might pump in the car on the drive in or on the subway (rock on mama!) Then at work they would have a morning pump session, a lunch session, and an early afternoon session or pump on the way home. This takes advantage of the commuting time. It really depends when you leave home and when you leave work. The basic idea is to pump every three hours.

Chapter 28

Breast Pumps

THE BEST PUMP FOR you depends on your scenario at work. There are all kinds of pumps (see the pros and cons section below), these are just a few examples of pumps mothers have mentioned they like.

Elvie

Pros:

- Hands free, wearable, slides into your bra
- No tubing
- Quietest
- 2 flange sizes included in box (24 mm, 28 mm). Can buy 21 mm.

- Smart, connects to phone app to monitor and track volumes
- Collects up to 5 ounces of milk (150 cc)
- 5 parts to clean – not too bad

Cons:

- Cost – single costs $279, double costs $499
- Hard to get, often on backorder. Easier to get if you live in the UK
- Reported to leak if you lean over

Willow

Pros:

- Hands free, wearable, slides into your bra
- No tubing
- Quieter
- Reusable container option

Cons:

- Cost – double costs $499
- Disposable bag option. Some reuse them but many purchase bags for each pumping session ($23.99 for 48 bags)
- Environmental impact of the bags if not reused
- Willow 1 bag capacity is only 4 ounces (120 cc). Willow 2 bag capacity is 5 ounces (150cc). May not be best pump for large-busted women
- Makes a loud noise when the bag is full

Baby Buddha

Pros:

- Hands free – wear the pump around your neck hanging from a lanyard
- Strong suction
- Can use with closed Freemie cups (hold 8 ounces, 240 cc per cup) – Cost of Freemies about $60

- Cost of Baby Buddha is about $200

Cons:

- Tubing to deal with
- Hard to hide it all
- Some noise

Consider

- Baby Buddha pump with closed system Freemies. The Baby Buddha is small and hangs on a lanyard around your neck. It connects via tubes to the Freemies that cup your breast and the milk collects in a container that is within the Freemie (like the size of a big orange). This hands-free approach allows you to walk around and do things while you are pumping.

Spectra 1 Plus, Spectra 2 Plus, Spectra 9 Plus (people often leave off the Plus when talking about these pumps)

Pros:

- Spectra 1 has a battery, so it is rechargeable.
- Spectra 2 is same as 1 but without the rechargeable battery.
- Spectrum 9 is small enough to put into a pocket.
- Efficient suction
- With a slight hack, can use with closed Freemie system
- Cost – S1 about $200, S2 about $150, S9 about $170

Cons:

- Spectra 1 and 2 are not for walking around
- Tubing

Consider:

- Spectra 1 with closed system Freemies. You pump while you are in your car driving into work; the milk will go into the

Freemie cup. Then you pour the milk out into a container and place it in a cool space to await transport home.

Medela Pump In Style
Pros:
- It's fine
- Cost is about $190

Cons:
- Tubing

Cleaning all the stuff

You can pump and then put the collection system unwashed (not the actual pump) into a Ziploc bag in the fridge. Then reuse it each time you pump and repeat. Only wash it once a day – perhaps when you get home.

Storage

You are going to need either a cooler with ice or a freezer pack or a fridge to store the pumped milk in at work. Milk is good in the fridge for up to 8 days. The rule is: smell it, if it smells ok it is good to use.

The best milk is fresh "from the tap" or directly from the breast. The next best milk is milk that has been in the fridge. The next best milk is milk from the freezer.

Time and space, it's the law

The Affordable Care Act requires employers to provide "reasonable break time for an employee to express breast milk for her nursing child for one year after the child's birth each time such employee has need to express the milk."

Employers are also required to provide "a place, other than a bathroom, that is shielded from view and free from intrusion from coworkers and the public, which may be used by an employee to express breast milk."

All employers covered by the Fair Labor Standards Act (FLSA) must comply with break time for the nursing mother's provision unless they have fewer than 50 employees and can demonstrate that compliance with the provision would impose an undue hardship.

This break time requirement became effective when the Affordable Care Act was signed into law on March 23, 2010.

Plan ahead! It's a good idea to let your employer know that when you return to work you will need 20-30-minute breaks in your schedule to allow for pumping time. Also ask about the lactation space. Remember, this is a law. Time and space are your right.

Information from Nancy Mohrbacher website, Dr. Milk Facebook group posts, and www.Kellymom.com.

Chapter 29

Lactation Cookies

LACTATION COOKIES CAN HELP increase the mother's milk production.

Oatmeal Chocolate Chip
Lactation Cookies / recipe by Noel Trujillo

Ingredients

- 1 cup butter (let it sit out to soften)
- 1 cup sugar
- 1 cup firmly packed brown sugar
- 4 tablespoons water
- 2 tablespoons flax seed meal
- 2 eggs
- 1 teaspoon vanilla
- 3 cups flour
- 1 teaspoon baking soda
- 1 teaspoon salt
- 3 cuts oats
- 1 cup chocolate chips
- You could add 3 tablespoons of peanut butter and use peanut butter chips instead of chocolate
- 2-4 tablespoons brewer's yeast (not bitter)

Preparation

1. Preheat oven to 350 degrees
2. Mix the flaxseed meal and water and let sit for 3-5 minutes
3. Beat butter, sugar, and brown sugar well
4. Add eggs and mix well
5. Add flaxseed mix and vanilla, beat well
6. Stir together flour, brewer's yeast, baking soda and salt
7. Add dry ingredients to butter mix
8. Stir in oats and chips
9. Scoop onto baking sheet
10. Bake for 12 minutes
11. Let set for a couple minutes and then remove from the tray

If you want to increase the supply more you can use more brewer's yeast or oatmeal.

Ready in 27 minutes

Makes 4 ½ dozen

Major Milk Makin' Lactation Cookies / recipe by Kathleen Major

Ingredients

- 1½ cup whole wheat flour
- 1¾ cup oats
- 1 teaspoon baking soda
- 1 teaspoon salt
- ¾ cup almond butter or peanut butter
- ½ cup butter, softened
- 1 cup milled flax
- 3 tablespoons brewer's yeast
- 1/3 cup water
- 1 teaspoon cinnamon
- ½ cup sugar
- ½ cup brown sugar
- 1 teaspoon vanilla
- 2 large eggs
- 2 cups (12 oz.) chocolate chips
- 1 cup chopped nuts of your choice

Preparation

1. Preheat oven to 350 degrees
2. Combine flour, baking soda, cinnamon and salt in a bowl
3. In a large bowl, beat almond butter, butter, sugar, brown sugar, vanilla, brewer's yeast, flax and water until creamy
4. Mix in eggs

5. Gradually beat in flour mixture
6. Mix in nuts and chocolate chips
7. Add oats slowly, mixing along the way
8. Place balls of dough onto greased baking sheets or baking stones
9. Press down each ball lightly with a fork
10. Bake 12 minutes
11. Allow to cool
12. Enjoy!

Adelyn's Favorite

Ingredients

- 1 cup old-fashioned oatmeal
- ½ cup of peanut butter (creamy)
- ½ cup ground flaxseed (can put in some whole for the crunch
- 1 cup shredded coconut (sweetened)
- 1/3 cup of honey
- ½ tablespoon brewer's yeast (can double this if you like)
- 1 teaspoon vanilla
- ½ cup mini chocolate chips (semisweet Ghirardelli)

Preparation

1. Combine the dry ingredients first: oatmeal, coconut, chocolate chips, brewer's yeast, and flax seed
2. Add the peanut butter, honey and vanilla and stir together
3. Refrigerate at least one hour
4. Remove from the refrigerator and roll the mixture into small balls

Chapter 30

Starting Solids

AT AROUND SIX MONTHS of age it's time to consider starting solid foods. The baby is developmentally ready for solids if:

- The tongue thrust is gone
- He or she can sit up
- There is good head control
- Seems interested when others are eating

The order is breast milk first and solids second. At this age, most calories are still coming from breast milk. Remember, food before one is mostly just for fun! Food also helps the baby develop hand eye coordination, work on textures, and try different tastes.

The traditional way of introducing solids is to give an iron-fortified cereal mixed with breast milk first – then adding a little fruit. An adult feeds the baby the bowl full of mushy food with a spoon. Eventually, two bowls of mushy, iron-fortified cereal are given perhaps at breakfast and dinner time. Pureed vegetables and then meats can be added maybe at lunchtime. Start with one meal a day and then work up to three meals a day.

Another way to introduce solids is to offer iron-rich foods using a method first described in a book by Gill Rapely called Baby-Led Weaning (BLW). The idea is to let the baby finger feed foods that the family is eating or bring a spoonful of soft food to the mouth by themselves.

Concerns about BLW include the risk of choking and developing iron deficiency anemia.

This baby is practicing her hand/eye coordination skills.

Section 4

That's a Wrap

CHAPTER 31

Appendix: Terms

APNO (All Purpose Nipple Ointment)

THIS IS AN OINTMENT that contains three different ingredients: 1) antibacterial 2) steroid 3) antifungal. It is made in a compounding pharmacy. It can be applied twice a day to the mother's nipples but long-term use is not recommended due to the steroid. Don't forget that the key to sore nipples is to fix the latch!

APNO contains:

- Mupirocin ointment (2%) 15 grams
- Betamethasone ointment (0.1%) 15 grams
- Miconazole powder added to a concentration of 2% miconazole

Devices to catch the dripping milk on the non-nursing breast.

Haakaa – This silicone device is placed on the non-nursing breast when the baby is feeding to collect leaking milk. Suction can be applied which pulls out more milk. The milk can be saved and used later on.

Milkies Milk-Saver – Slide this into the bra on the non-nursing side and collect leaking breast milk as you nurse.

Sore Nipples – Things to try to soothe and heal sore nipples include: breast milk, lanolin, Medihoney, or Motherlove. I think expressed breast milk should be tried first. Lanolin has been used for years to treat sore nipples. It is a greasy yellow substance made from secretions (sebum) from the skin glands of sheep to condition their wool. It is a natural, animal-derived product harvested from shorn wool. Refined lanolin has been used for more than a hundred years in ointments. Because of its high fat content, lanolin is occlusive – it prevents the evaporation of water from the skin. This keeps skin moisturized and helps the skin heal. Medihoney contains a beeswax but there is no concern about botulism affecting the baby because the spores have been gamma irradiated, so inactivated and killed.

SNS (supplemental nursing system)

A supplemental nursing system is a device that allows the baby to get supplemental nutrition (mother's expressed milk, donor milk, infant formula) while nursing. There are brand name SNS devices. In our hospital we make our own by attaching a feeding tube to a small syringe. The syringe is filled with the supplement and then the end of the tube slides into the corner of the baby's mouth. Pressing on the syringe, the supplement is slowly dripped into the baby's mouth while he is nursing.

Triple Feeds

Triple feeding means you do three things every time you feed your baby – nurse, pump and bottle feed.

- Feed the baby at the breast to keep the baby breast oriented and the body stimulated
- Then pump
- Then feed the baby the pumped breast milk (and more if needed) by a bottle

IBCLC

This stands for International Board Certified Lactation Consultant and is the gold standard credential. A candidate can choose from one of three pathways. For all three pathways, to qualify to take the exam, candidates must complete a minimum of 90 hours of lactation education, specified general education in the health sciences, many hours of clinical experience in providing lactation and breastfeeding care, and adherence to the Code of Professional Conduct for IBCLCs. Recertification is required every five years.

Numerous certificate programs exist (information from Motherlove February 20, 2018 post)

- CLC – Certified Lactation Counselor. The certification is given upon completion of a five-day training course offered by the Healthy Children Project Center for Breastfeeding. It also requires passing a written examination at the end of the course.

- CLS – Certified Lactation Specialist. Completed a 5-day course.

- CLE – Certified Lactation Educator. Completed a 20-hour breastfeeding training course and passed a final online exam.

- CBC – Certified Breastfeeding Counselor. Completed a mentored online training course and have provided 30 hours of breastfeeding support.

- LEC – Lactation Educator Counselor. These are typically health professionals who have received five days of on-site or online education and training and satisfactorily completed periodic testing.

Chapter 32

References

Position Statements

- American Academy of Pediatrics. Section on Breastfeeding. Breastfeeding and the Use of Human Milk. *Pediatrics.* 2012;129:e827-841.

- ACOG. Committee Opinion. Optimizing Support for Breastfeeding as Part of Obstetric Practice. Number 658. February 2016

- American Academy of Family Physicians. Breastfeeding, Family Physicians Supporting (Position Paper). 2014 http://www.aafp.org/about/policies/all/breastfeeding-support.html

Excellent Resources

- Ruth A. Lawrence and Robert M. Lawrence. *Breastfeeding: A Guide for the Medical Profession.* 7th Edition. Copyright 2011 by Mosby, and imprint of Elsevier, Inc.

- Amy Brown. *Breastfeeding Uncovered: Who really decides how we feed our babies.* Pinter and Martin Ltd 2016

- Amy Brown. *The Positive Breastfeeding Book: Everything you need to feed your baby with confidence.* Pinter and Martin Ltd 2018

- Nancy Mohrbacher and Kathleen Kendall-Tackett. *Breastfeeding Made Simple: Seven Natural Laws for Nursing Mothers.* New Harbinger Publications, Inc. 5674 Shattuck

Avenue, Oakland CA. 2010

- Jack Newman. *Breastfeeding: Empowering Parents.* International Breastfeeding Center. 2018. www.ibconline.ca
- Ed Yong. Breastfeeding the Microbiome. *The New Yorker.* July 22, 2016

Skin-to-Skin Contact

- Feldman-Winter L, Goldsmith JP. AAP Committee on Fetus and Newborn, Task Force on Sudden Infant Death Syndrome. *Pediatrics.* 2016;138(3):e20161889.
- Phillips R. The Sacred Hour: Uninterrupted skin-to-skin contact immediately after birth. *Newborn and Infant Nursing Reviews.* 2013;13:67-72
- Davanzo R, De Cunto A, Paviotti G, et al. Making the first days of life safer: preventing sudden unexpected postnatal collapse while promoting breastfeeding. *J Hum Lact.* 2015;31(1):47-52.
- Dani C, Cecchi A, Commare A, et al. Behavior of the newborn during skin-to-skin. *J Hum Lact.* Aug 2015;31(3):452-457.
- Steven J, et al. *Maternal and Child Nutrition.* 2014;10:456-473.
- Merewood A. Skin-to-skin at birth: A new model of care. *J Hum Lact.* November 2014;30:509-510. Inside Track

Rooming-In

- Feldman-Winter L, Goldsmith JP. AAP Committee on Fetus and Newborn, Task Force on Sudden Infant Death Syndrome. *Pediatrics.* 2016;138(3):e20161889.
- Holmes AV, McLeod AY, Bunik M. Academy of Breastfeeding Medicine Clinical Protocol #5: Peripartum Breastfeeding Management for the Healthy Mother and Infant at Term, Revision 2013. Academy of breastfeeding medicine/protocols (https://www.bfmed.org/protocols)
- DiGirolamo AM, Grummer-Strawn LM, Fein SB. Effect of maternity-care practices on breastfeeding. *Pediatrics.*

2008;122 (Suppl 2);S43-S49.

- Murry EK, Ricketts S, Dellaport J. Hospital practices that increase breastfeeding duration: results from a population-based study. *Birth*. 2007;34(3):202-211.
- Ball HL, Ward-Platt MP, Heslop E, et al. Randomised trial of infant sleep location on the postnatal ward. *Arch Dis Child*. 2006;91(12):1005-1010.

Breastfeeding is Analgesic

- Gray L, Miller LW, Philipp BL, Blass EM. Breastfeeding is analgesic in health newborns. *Pediatrics* 2002;109(4):590-3. (Breastfeeding can act as a pain killer , an analgesic, when newborns are pricked in the heel to obtain blood for the newborn metabolic screen. The authors of a 2002 study found that crying and grimacing was essentially eliminated in babies who were breastfeeding while undergoing heel sticks. In addition, breastfeeding prevented the marked increase in heart rate that normally happens during the heel stick procedure. Because of these findings, mothers should consider breastfeeding the baby during any heel stick procedures.)

The Baby-Friendly Hospital Initiative

- Merewood A, Bugg K, Burnham L, et al. Addressing racial inequities in breastfeeding in the southern United States. *Pediatrics*. 2019; 143(2):e20181897.
- WHO, UNICEF. Protecting, promoting, and supporting breastfeeding in facilities providing maternity and newborn services: The revised Baby-Friendly Hospital Initiative 2018 / Implementation Guidance www.who.int/nutrition/publications/infantfeeding/bfhi-implementation/en/
- Chantry CJ, et al. In hospital formula use increases early breastfeeding cessation among first tie mothers intending to exclusively breastfeed. *J Pediatrics*. 2014;164:1339-1345.
- Martis R, Stufkens J. The New Aealand/Aotearoa Baby-Friendly Hospital Initiative Implementation Journey: Piki Ake Te Tihi – "Strive for Excellence." *J Hum Lact*. 2013;29(2);140-146.

- Hansen MN, Baerug A, Nylander G, et al. Challenges and successes: The Baby-Friendly Initiative in Norway. *J Hum Lact.* 2012;28(3):285-288.
- Grguric J, Wen RA, Kylberg E, et al. International perspectives on the Baby-Friendly Initiative. *J Hum Lact.* 2012;28(3):281-284.
- Labbok MH. Global Baby-Friendly Hospital Initiative monitoring data: update and discussion. *Breastfeeding Med.* 2012;7(4);210-222.
- Saadeh RJ. The Baby-Friendly Hospital Initiative 20 years on: facts, progress and the way forward. *J Hum Lact.* 2012;28(3):271-275.
- Bartick M, Stuebe AM, Shealy KR, et al. Closing the quality gap: Promoting evidence-based breastfeeding care in the hospital. *Pediatrics.* 2009;124(Supplement).
- Merten S, et al. Do Baby-Friendly hospitals influence breastfeeding duration on a national level? *Pediatrics.* 2005;116:e701-e708.
- Kramer MS, Chalmers B, Hodnett ED, et al. Promotion of breastfeeding intervention trial (PROBIT): a randomized trial in the Republic of Belarus. *JAMA.* 2001;285;413.

Does Baby-Friendly Work?

Agency for Healthcare Research (AHRQ)

- Feltner C et al. Breastfeeding Programs and Policies, Breastfeeding Uptake, and Maternal Health Outcomes in Developed Countries. Comparative Effectiveness Review No. 210. AHRQ Publication No. 18-EHC014-EF. July 18, 2018. The purpose of this systemic review was to "summarize the effectiveness of community, workplace, and health care system–based programs and policies aimed at supporting and promoting breastfeeding, and to determine the association between breastfeeding and maternal health." The study concludes that the Baby-Friendly Hospital Initiative (BFHI) is associated with improved rates of breastfeeding initiation and duration.

The Lancet Breastfeeding Series

- Victora CG, Bahl R, Barros AJ, et al; Lancet Breastfeeding Series Group. Breastfeeding in the 21st century: epidemiology, mechanisms, and lifelong effect. *Lancet.* 2016;387:475-490.

- Rollins NC, Bhandari N, Hajeebhoy N, et al; Lancet Breastfeeding Series Group. Why invest, and what it will take to improve breastfeeding practices? *Lancet.* 2016;387:491-504. A meta-analysis of studies evaluating the BFHI found that implementation of the BFHI increased exclusive breastfeeding by 49% (95% CI, 33%-68%) and any breastfeeding by 66% (95% CI, 34%-107%). The meta-analysis reviewed 29 studies that found that the BFHI and its elements of hospital support increased breastfeeding in the first hour (relative risk = 1.11; 95% CI, 1.06-1.16), 51 studies that found that it increased exclusive breastfeeding in the first 5 months (relative risk 1.46; 95% CI, 1.37-1.56), and 47 studies that found that it increased any breastfeeding in the first 6 months (relative risk 1.40; 95% CI, 1.30-1.52).

- Authors propose 6 action points: 1) Disseminate the evidence; 2) Foster positive societal attitudes towards breastfeeding; 3) Show political will; 4) Regulate the breast milk-substitute industry; 5) Scale up and monitor breastfeeding interventions and trends in breastfeeding practices; and 6) For political institutions to exercise their authority and remove structural and societal barriers that hinder women's ability to breastfeed.

Best Fed Beginnings

- Feldman-Winter L, Ustianov J, Anastasio J, et al. Best Fed Beginnings: A nationwide quality improvement initiative to increase breastfeeding. *Pediatrics.* 2017;140(1):e20163121. This study found that for hospitals in this initiative, overall breastfeeding increased from 79% to 83% (t=1.93; P=.057) and exclusive breastfeeding increased from 39% to 61% (t=9.72; P=<.001)

Boston Medical Center

- Parker M, Burnham L, Cook J, Sanchez E, Philipp BL, Merewood A. Ten years after Baby-Friendly designation: Breastfeeding rates continue to increase in a US neonatal intensive care unit. *J Hum Lact.* 2013;29(3): 354-358.

- Merewood A, Mehta SD, Chamberlain LB, Philipp BL, Bauchner H. Breastfeeding rates in US Baby-Friendly hospital: Results of a national survey. *Pediatrics.* 2005; 116(3):628-634.

- Philipp BL, Malone KL, Cimo S, Merewood A. Sustained breastfeeding grates at a US Baby-Friendly hospital. *Pediatrics.* 2003;112(3):e234-e236.

- Merewood A, Philipp BL, Chawla N, Cimo S. The Baby-Friendly Hospital Initiative increases breastfeeding rates in a US neonatal intensive care unit. *J Hum Lact.* 2003;19(2):166-171.

- Philipp BL, Merewood A, Miller LW, et al. Baby-Friendly Hospital Initiative improves breastfeeding initiation rates in a US hospital setting. *Pediatrics.* 2001;108(3):677-681.

The Ten Steps and Breastfeeding Exclusivity

- Kahin SA, McGurk M, Hansen-Smith H, et al. Key program findings and insights from the Baby-Friendly Hawaii Project. *J Hum Lact.* First published Jan 30, 2017.

- Declercq E, Labbok MH, Sakala C, O'Hara M. Hospital practices and women's likelihood of fulfilling their intention to exclusively breastfeed. *Am J Public Health.* May 2009;99;5:929-935.

- Merten S, Dratva J, Ackermann-Liebrich U. Do baby-friendly hospitals influence breastfeeding duration on a national level? *Pediatrics.* 2005;116;5:e702-708.

- Martens PJ. Does breastfeeding education affect nursing staff beliefs, exclusive breastfeeding rates, and Baby-Friendly Hospital Initiative compliance? The experience of a small, rural Canadian hospital. *J Hum Lact.* 2000;16;4:309-318

The Ten Steps and Breastfeeding Duration

- Garcia-de-Leon-Gonzalez R, Oliver-Roig A, Hernandez-Martinez M, et al. Becoming baby-friendly in Spain: A quality-improvement process. *Acta Paediatr.* 2011;100;3:445-450.

- DiGirolamo AM, Grummer-Strawn LM, Fein SB. Effect of maternity-care practices on breastfeeding. *Pediatrics.* 2008;122 Suppl 2:S43-49.

- Rosenberg KD, Stull JD, Adler MR, et al. Impact of hospital policies on breastfeeding outcomes. *Breastfeeding Medicine.* 2008; 3: 110-6.

- Merten S, Dratva J and Ackermann-Liebrich U. Do baby-friendly hospitals influence breastfeeding duration on a national level? *Pediatrics.* 2005; 116: e702-8.

- Murray E. Hospital practices that increase breastfeeding-duration: results from a population based study. *Birth.* 2006; 34: 202-10.

- DiGirolamo AM, Grummer-Strawn LM, Fein S. Maternity care practices: Implications for breastfeeding. *Birth.* 2001;28;2:94-100.

- Luddington-Hoe SM, Morgan K. Infant assessment and reduction of sudden unexpected postnatal collapse risk during skin-to-skin contact. *Newborn and Infant Nursing Reviews.* 2014;14:28-33.

- Barbero P, Madamangalam AS, Shields A. Skin to skin after Cesarean birth. *J Hum Lact.* November 2013:29:446-448.

- Moore ET, et al. Cochrane Database Syst Rev. 2012;5:CDOO3519

- Bramson L, Lee JW, Moore E, et al. Effect of early infant skin-to-skin mother-baby contact during the first 3 hours following birth on exclusive breastfeeding during the maternity hospital stay. *J Hum Lact.* 2010;26(2):130-137.

Industry Sponsored Diaper Discharge Bags and Breastfeeding

- Nelson JM, Li R, Perrine CG. Trends of US hospitals

distributing infant formula packs to breastfeeding mothers, 2007 to 2013. *Pediatrics.* 2015;135(6);1051-1056.

- Public Citizen. Top Hospitals' Formula for Success: No Marketing of Infant Formula. October 2013.
- Delaware Bans Hospital Gift Bags of Baby Formula. Delaware Public Media. July 23, 2015.
- Maryland Bans the Bags. Ban the Bags Website. October 2015.
- Rosenberg KD, Eastham CA, Kasehagen LJ, et al. Marketing infant formula through hospitals: the impact of commercial hospital discharge packs on breastfeeding. *Am J Public Health.* 2008;98(2):290-295.
- Donnelly A, Snowden HM, Renfrew MJ, et al. Commercial hospital discharge packs for breastfeeding women. Cochrane Data Base Systematic Review. 2000;2: CD002075.
- Perez-Escamilla R, Pollitt E, Lonnerdal B, et al. Infant feeding policies in maternity wards and their effect on breast-feeding success: an analytical overview. *Am J of Public Health.* 1994;84(1), 89.

Banning the Bags

In 2007, according to a national survey conducted by the CDC, 70% of US maternity facilities distributed formula-company sponsored diaper bags to new mothers when they left the hospital, a violation of the Code. The formula company gave these bags to the hospital for free. While these bags may appear to be a thoughtful gift to the family, they are actually part of a marketing scheme designed to influence mothers to choose that particular brand of formula. Distribution of this free bag by the nurse and doctor implies their 'seal of approval' to the product. Distribution of these diaper bags has been shown to undermine breastfeeding success, even when the formula is removed from the bag. Women given these products are less likely to breastfeed exclusively compared to women who do not take home the bags.

More hospitals are now banning the bags. In 2013, 30% were distributing the bags, down from the 70% in 2007. Public

Citizen reported in April 2016 that 95% of the largest US public hospitals had banned the bags.

In 2011, Rhode Island became the first state in the union to ban the bags. Massachusetts followed in 2012 when all 49 maternity facilities in the Bay State banned the bags. Following a celebration at the State House, leaders of the initiative travelled to the site of the Boston Tea Party for a ceremonial (and pretend) tossing of the bags into the Boston Harbor (pictures below).

Delaware, Maryland, New Hampshire and West Virginia have also banned the bags. Cities are leading the way as well: Washington DC is Bag Free as are Philadelphia and Detroit. A website, banthebags.com, tracks progress in the Ban the Bag movement.

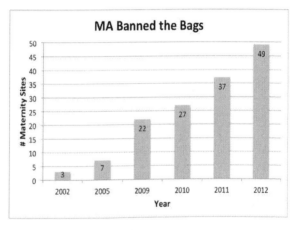

Economic Factors Associated with Breastfeeding

- Bartick M, Reinhold A. The burden of suboptimal breastfeeding in the United States: A pediatric cost analysis. *Pediatrics.* 2010; 125(5):e1048-e1056. "**Results:** If 90% of US families could comply with medical recommendations to breastfeed exclusively for 6 months, the United States would save $13 billion per year and prevent an excess of 911 deaths, nearly all of which would be in infants ($10.5 billion and 741 deaths at 80% compliance)."

- Bartick M, Stuebe AM, Schwarz EB, et al. Cost analysis of maternal disease associated with suboptimal breastfeeding. *Obstetrics and Gynecology.* 2013;122(1):111-119.

- "Results: If observed associations between breastfeeding duration and maternal health are causal, we estimate that current breastfeeding rates result in 4,981 excess cases of breast cancer, 53,847 cases of hypertension, and 13,946 cases of myocardial infarction compared with a cohort of 1.88 million U.S. women who optimally breastfed. Using a 3% discount rate, suboptimal breastfeeding incurs a total of $17.4 billion in cost to society resulting from premature death (95% confidence interval [CI] $4.38–24.68 billion), $733.7 million in direct costs (95% CI $612.9–859.7 million), and $126.1 million indirect morbidity costs (95% CI $99.00–153.22 million). We found a nonsignificant difference in number of deaths before age 70 years under current breastfeeding rates (4,396 additional premature deaths, 95% CI: 810–7,918)."

Maternal Factors and Breastfeeding

- Schwarz EB, Ray RM, Stuebe AM, et al. Duration of lactation and risk factors for maternal cardiovascular disease. *Obstetrics and Gynecology.* 2009;113(5):974-982.

- Stuebe AM, et al. Nurses Health Study. *Am J Obstet Gynecol.* 2009;200:138.e1-8.

- Schwarz EB, McClure CK, Tepper PG, et al. Lactation and maternal measures of subclinical cardiovascular disease. *Obstetrics and Gynecology.* 2010;115(1):41-48.

- Meek JY, Noble L. Implementation of the Ten Steps saves lives. *JAMA Pediatr.* 2016;170(10)

- Patnode CD, Henninger ML, Senger CA, et al. Primary care interventions to support breastfeeding: evidence report and systematic review for the US Preventative Services Task Force. *JAMA.* doi:10.1001/JAMA. 2016.8882

- Flaherman V, Von Kohorn I. (Editorial) Interventions intended to support breastfeeding. Updated assessment of benefits and harm. *JAMA.* 2016;316(16):1685-1687.

- Bartick MC, Nickel NC, Hanley LE. Evidence for the Baby-Friendly Hospital Intervention to support breastfeeding. *JAMA.* 2017;317(7):770-771.

- Bass J, Gartley T, Kleinman R. (Viewpoint) Unintended consequences of current breastfeeding initiatives. *JAMA Pediatr.* 2016;170(10):923-924.

- Omission of Conflict of Interest Disclosures. *JAMA Pediatr.* 2017;17(4):399

- Bartick M. Influential article against Baby-Friendly is based on a false claim. *Huff Post.* November 25, 2017.

- The Importance of the Baby-Friendly Hospital Initiative.

1. Gartner LM, Brownlee A, MacEnroe PT. *JAMA Pediatr.* 2017;171(3):302-303 (Baby-Friendly USA)

2. Boyd L, Kowalska M, Askew GL. *JAMA Pediatr.* 2017;171(3):303-303. (New York City Department of Health)

3. Ferrarello D. *JAMA Pediatr.* 2017;171(3):303-304. (United States Lactation Consultant Association)

4. Walker M. *JAMA Pediatr.* 2017;171(3):304-304. (National Alliance for Breastfeeding Advocacy)

5. Wasser HM, Heinig MJ, Tully KP. *JAMA Pediatr.* 2017;171(3):304-305. (UNC Chapel Hill and UC Davis)

6. Philipp BL. *JAMA Pediatr.* 2017;171(3):305-305 (Boston University School of Medicine)

7. Bass JL, Gartley T, Kleinman R. *JAMA Pediatr.* 2017;171(3):305-306. (In reply)

CHAPTER 33

About the Author

BARBARA L. PHILIPP, MD, is a pediatrician, breastfeeding expert, and Professor of Pediatrics at Boston University School of Medicine. As Pediatric Medical Director of the Mother Baby Unit at her hospital for more than a decade and now as a member of the Division of Newborn Medicine attending team, Dr. Philipp estimates she has cared for more than 20,000 newborns. Working on the frontlines, she sees the joys and hardships new mothers face every day.

A Fellow of the American Academy of Pediatrics and of the Academy of Breastfeeding Medicine, Dr. Philipp is a firm believer in the importance of breastfeeding for the mother and her baby through the first year of the baby's life. She is also acutely aware of how difficult breastfeeding can be for many women. Dr. Philipp believes that our hospitals, culture and politics are miserably failing us when it comes to breastfeeding.

From routine separation of mothers and new babies in many maternity hospitals, to staff with little or no training in breastfeeding, to formula sales representatives roaming the halls of maternity units and cutting backdoor deals with hospitals, Dr. Philipp has seen it all. Now she's on a mission to empower new mothers and fathers with the information they need to make informed decisions about what to look for in a hospital, what to demand from hospital staff, and how to meet a one-year breastfeeding goal.

Dr. Philipp has published numerous articles and lectures nationwide on breastfeeding related- topics. She is the author of a peer-reviewed, on-line breastfeeding training program that, in the two years since publication, has been viewed by over 1000 doctors, midwives and nurse practitioners.

Known to friends as Bobbi, Dr. Philipp lives in Lexington Massachusetts with her husband Vince. They have three children; twins Nick and Abby and oldest daughter, Jess, who's pregnancy served as the impetus for this book.

Made in the USA
Middletown, DE
22 September 2020

20343672R10094